SECRET SPAIN

Visit Alicante's Myths And Legends

Sarah Farrell

Legal Notices

No part of this publication may be reproduced or transmitted in any material form (including photocopying or storing in any medium by electronic means) without the written permission of the author ***

The purpose of this book is to educate, entertain and provide information on the subject matter covered. All attempts have been made to verify the information at the time of publication, and the author does not assume any responsibility for errors, omissions or other interpretations of the subject matter. The purchaser or reader of this book assumes responsibility for the use of this material and information. The author assumes no responsibility or liability on behalf of any purchaser or reader of this book.

DEDICATION

To my family, especially my Dad, Denis Farrell, who was an incredible journalist with a wonderful way with words. I hope I've inherited a smidgeon of his talent along with his dry sense of humour. He was kind enough to pass on his passion for Charlton Athletic.

Additional thanks to: -

Illustrator: Younesselh for my beautiful book cover

Editor and book coach: Dale Darley of Book Brand Business and Write With Dale without whom this book would still be stuck on my endless To Do List. Thank you for your patience, inspiration and encouragement.

Spain: For the most amazing history, myths, legends, stories and photo opportunities.

TABLE OF CONTENTS

Introduction

Spain is amazing. Ask people what Spain means to them and they'll probably mention flamenco, paella, Benidorm, bull-fighting, beaches and sunshine. They may also mention Dali and Picasso. But Spain is way more exciting than that.

What about the fiestas? Cuisine? History? Culture? Legends? Miracles? Myths? Seemingly every small town and village has its own fiesta but we only get to hear about a handful of them or because we just happen to be in town at the right time.

I'll be the first to hold my hand up and say 'that's me!'. The first year I moved to Spain, I walked out of a bar and slap-bang into the middle of a huge, noisy parade. "What's this?" I asked the bartender. "It's the Moors and Christians fiesta."

I duly found out as much as I could about the Moors and Christians in Spain. And that's where the idea for this book came from. To share some of these beautiful traditions with you. So you get to know another side to Spain. A side which is very magical.

Instead of stumbling across something fascinating and amazing during your trip to Spain or, worse still, coming home without discovering them, you can enjoy this voyage into Alicante's amazing past. Get to know its heritage and legendary tales to enhance your experience and see the region in a fresh new light.

Together, we will see just how tremendously amazing Spain truly is. I'm so excited to share just a teeny, tiny part of the legends and oral traditions with you.

For this first Secret Spain book I've focused on the area I know and love the best, the Alicante province. I'm so thrilled you'll be sharing this journey with me. First we'll embark on an imaginary journey through the stories of the Moors in Alicante. The Moors ruled many parts of Spain for 800 years from 711 to 1492. Some areas were under Moorish rule for longer than others. But their legacy lives on today in the crops they brought from their homeland including citrus fruits, vines and rice; their irrigation methods; the beautiful castles they built in Spain; and their legendary tales.

In the final chapter, Chapter 12, you can read a very short history of how the Moors conquered Spain. How the Christians regained power. And about the amazing Moors and Christians fiesta reenacting the battles between the two warring parties.

This book invites you to go on an imaginary journey, time-travelling back into a small part of Spain's incredible history. After each legendary tale is a guide to the towns where these events happened – Alicante, Guardamar del Segura and Rojales, Orihuela, Alcoy and Jalón Valley.

After reading these tales, when you travel to the destinations in this book, you'll see evidence of the Moorish legacy for yourself - in the buildings, street names and cuisine. You'll feel these stories come to life as you stand in the spot where these wonderful tales took place.

You're about to go on a journey through Spain's rich past. It will take you along the Costa Blanca coast and into the glorious mountains of inland Alicante. I hope you enjoy this journey as much as I have. You can experience a totally different side to Spain. Each destination can be visited individually as a day trip or enjoy a road trip lasting several days starting and ending in Alicante.

You can read the chapters in any order. Start with the one that intrigues you the most. Or the town you'd most love to visit.

Enjoy this amazing adventure in this beautiful part of Spain.

Chapter 1: Why is a Moor's face etched in the side of Alicante Castle?

If you stand by Postiguet beach, turn your back to the sea and look up, you'll see the face of a Moorish ruler's sadness etched in the rocks. And if you listen very closely you'll hear the desperate pleas of a young and beautiful Princess. Let's find out more about her.

"He has to win, he has to win," cried Princess Cantara to no one in particular, hoping her wishes could be carried on the breeze to arrive at their rightful destination. Signed, sealed and delivered with love. She felt a blush rising from her pounding heart at the thought of her beloved and extremely romantic love, Ali. The young Moor's poetry filled her soul with hope in every stanza. Each line forged an unbreakable link between their hearts.

Just a short time earlier her father, the Caliph, had decided in all of his wisdom to set a task for two handsome suitors to win the hand of his daughter Cantara.

Cantara reminded him of his wife and the tests that he had

to endure to win her heart. His thoughts often travelled to his dark and gracious wife, who'd bestowed her shining raven hair and dark eyes on their favourite child.

No one would claim his daughter and a place at his table in the grand hall at Santa Bárbara Castle without first proving his worth. It was a magnificent castle, the envy of every Caliph around. Indeed, it was said to be one of the finest castles in the whole of Spain. But that meant nothing to Cantara at that moment.

"I am a Princess, I should marry whoever I wish," thought Cantara petulantly, as she looked out over the Mediterranean from her hiding post at the top of the castle.

"Why has my father set up this stupid task and put me up as the prize? What does he think I am? A trophy to be handed over to the man my father declares to be the winner?"

Cantara sighed so sorrowfully, the sparrows stop singing in their nests around the turret and turned towards the beautiful young woman.

She sighed again as she thought of her formidable father. He took his duties very seriously. He was not going to give his daughter's hand in marriage to the first man who declared he loves her. Unfortunately for Cantara, that meant Ali had some serious work to do before becoming her beloved husband. The thought of marrying Ali sent goosebumps shivering from her dainty feet to the top of her head. Suddenly, despite the sun's rays beating down, Cantara felt cold. Very cold and a little afraid.

Almanzor, a brave general from Cordoba, had also taken up the Caliph's challenge. On his travels, he'd heard whispers that the most beautiful young woman in Spain was ready to be married off. He loved a challenge and changed his plans so he would be in Alicante to win such a coveted prize.

Almanzor was more mature than Ali. Worldly wise and brave. He was the hot favourite to win Cantara's hand in marriage. At such an alarming prospect, Cantara gagged. The thought of being tied in permanent wedlock to the serious general made her stomach turn.

"What if he wins and he wants us to live in Cordoba? What a frightful life for me," thought Cantara to herself.

Her thoughts flashed back to the meeting between her father and her two suitors only two hours before.

Her father had dressed to impress in his finest purple silk

tunic elaborately embroidered with gold thread. Standing before him, Cantara looked like a dainty little doll. The Caliph was two metres tall, muscular and very dark.

His baritone voice rumbled as deep as thunder as he put his arm around his daughter and said: "To win my daughter's hand in marriage, first you need to earn my blessing. I have a deep respect for the Roman god Hercules, who carried out his Twelve Labours and never balked from the task, no matter how impossible it might appear. That's why I'm setting you a Herculean task. But you get to choose what your task shall be. The one that impresses me the most will marry Cantara. Now choose your task."

Almanzor was the first to speak. He smiled confidently as he said he would set sail immediately for India and bring back the finest spices and silks, the likes of which had never been seen before. He'd built up a formidable reputation during his military career and was confident the young whippersnapper standing beside him could not choose such an impressive feat.

Ali might be young but he wasn't daft. He had a cunning plan that would keep him close to his one true love. He told the Caliph he would build a 30km-long ditch to bring water from

Tibi to the castle. Water was so much more useful than silks and spices that they'd never heard of.

Both men bowed deeply to the Caliph and his daughter before turning quickly on their heels, anxious to start their tasks.

Cantara recalled what her father said to her when he saw her jet-black eyes were filled with tears. "You need to have faith, my little one. If Ali's love for you is as strong as he claims, then he will make sure he wins this task," he said.

As a good Muslim, he knew Allah, the Almighty, had already chosen the right path for Cantara.

"I wish only for your happiness. The time will come when you will thank me for this," he gently added.

Her dimpled chin trembled as she whispered: "I hope so." Then she turned and went back to her hidey-hole at the very top of the castle.

Only two hours after that tense discussion the Princess felt so very much older and sadder as she sat in her favourite spot, safe within the thick castle walls.

A noise broke into her thoughts and Ali rushed to her side. They looked out to sea and laughed as they watched the distinguished general sail away in his wooden boat with seven sails.

"It'll take forever to get to India in that little boat," giggled Cantara, as she gazed up at Ali, her eyes filled with the love she dared not speak.

"If he gets there at all," replied her young suitor.

With each passing day, their love grew deeper. Each morning Ali greeted Cantara with a poem he had written declaring his true feelings. He was so very much in love he was unable to sleep and spent his nights fruitfully writing romantic sonnets. Every afternoon he brought the plumpest dates, juiciest figs and fresh mint tea for Cantara to enjoy while he sang his love songs.

They were so wrapped up in each other that everything else was brushed aside like an unwanted, unread book. They were

Impressive Santa Bárbara Castle in Alicante

young. They were so much in love that it hurt. They hated being apart. And when they were apart, they were thinking of the next time they could meet. Unfortunately for them, Ali's task was long forgotten.

One morning they were huddled together as usual in the western corner of the castle's keep when they heard Cantara's name echoing around the castle's thick walls.

Then they heard footsteps and Cantara's maidservant flurried into the hidey-hole. Her face was flushed and she couldn't speak for a moment after running all over the castle looking for the young lady. What she eventually said frightened Cantara more than her scariest nightmares on the darkest of nights.

"Cantara! Cantara! Come at once. Almanzor's ship is sailing into the harbour. Your father commands you to join him to see what treasures he's brought back with him."

Ali's heart literally stopped for a moment. He hunched over, choking back his fear. He felt a coldness like ice creep over him and he was shaking as if he'd been plunged into the castle's cold room where they stored the meat. The challenge. The stupid challenge. He was so wrapped up in love that the challenge had disappeared from his mind faster than Almanzor's ship.

"If the gallant general has accomplished his mission, I will lose Cantara and another man will be calling her his wife," Ali thought morosely.

His skin tightened and he felt even colder at the thought of Cantara and Almanzor together as husband and wife.

"Hurry, please come at once," said the breathless maidservant. "Your father will be so angry with me if I return without you."

As she spoke, the ship with seven sails passed by and saluted the castle with the boom of its cannon.

The Princess knew what she had to do. She stood up, turned away from the man she loved and walked away. You would have thought her shoes were made of lead as she slowly made her way down the steep hill, her shoulders drooped lower and lower with each step.

As she reached the harbour, a strange aroma caught the back of her throat. It was warming, exotic, rather thrilling. She saw wooden chests filled with yellow, golden and red spices. Lying next to them were delicate silks in the richest emerald greens, ruby reds, corn yellow, dusky rose, ivory and deep purples.

Almanzor had done exceedingly well. He had brought saffron

that looked as rich as spun gold. Cinnamon with the warmest fragrance and bags of pearly white rice, which he proclaimed to be the finest rice in all of India.

Cantara couldn't resist. She reached down and touched the silk. It was so cool. So beautiful. She snatched her hand back and put it over her mouth as she realised what this meant. Ali lost and she now belonged to Almanzor. She was his treasure.

As gracefully as she could muster, Cantara thanked the general for his noble quest. Then she turned and walked as quickly as she could back to her room. She couldn't face Ali now that all was lost.

It wasn't long before her father threw open her bedroom door. Firmly but quietly he said: "What a hero Almanzor has proven to be. You should be proud to call him your husband."

Cantara's beautiful eyes filled with tears and she begged and begged her father to change his mind. But he could not.

"I am the ruler and I will not lose face. I gave my word to Almanzor and I will keep it. He is a fine man and will make you a good husband," he said firmly but kindly.

Alone in her room, Cantara sobbed so hard and for so long that her tears could have filled the water canal her beloved Ali was supposed to have dug. Just when she thought life could not get any worse, grave news reached her about darling Ali.

In desperation Ali had ridden to Tibi to start digging his ravine.

When he realised his task was too arduous and that he'd left it far too late, he threw himself to the bottom of a ravine. Miraculously, and rather ironically, the impact of his body split the ground in two and water started spouting from what is known today as the Pantano de Tibi (Tibi marsh).

The Princess felt her heart crack in two. How could Ali leave her all alone? He knew she could not live without him. Would not live without him. And so she decided to join him in the next world.

She hurled herself into the sea from the Sierra de San Julian mountain in the hope of joining Ali in the next life. Today, this spot is known as El Salto de la Reina Mora – the Moor Queen's Jump.

Her father was heartbroken and fell into a deep depression from which he never recovered. He bore the guilt, the hurt and the heartache for the rest of his days. He didn't eat. He couldn't sleep. Soon after, he too died.

But all three have been immortalised in the wonderful beach city of Alicante.

Today you can see the Caliph's melancholy face engraved in the side of Monte Benacantil just beneath the castle. What Ali and Cantara could not have in life, they achieved in death. Alicante is a marriage of their names – Ali and Cantara – to ensure the lovers will stay together forever in the name of their beloved city.

Like Shakespeare's Romeo and Juliet set in romantic Italy, this tale of star-crossed lovers is a sad reflection on how strongly young people feel when they fall in love. How parents have their best interests at heart but whose actions can appear cruel and unjust.

Does love really conquer all? Certainly there are no winners in the legend of Ali and Cantara.

Should families talk more instead of dictating to their children?

If the Caliph had reasoned with Cantara, would she have listened?

Should you sacrifice everything for love? Or do things seem better after you've slept on them or talked them over?

No matter which direction you come from, you cannot miss the majestic sight of Santa Bárbara Castle sitting high at the top of Monte Benacantil to guide you in. This emblem of the city stands as a magnificent reminder of Alicante's rich history throughout the centuries.

Now let's take a tour of this beautiful little city to see the Caliph's grief etched into the rock and find out what other tempting delights are in store for us as we discover Alicante for ourselves.

Chapter 2: Amazing things to see and do in Alicante

Alicante is full of surprises. Turn a corner and find yourself in a lively traditional Spanish plaza or square with ornate cafés. Follow another path to find grand old trees with gnarly trunks. Turn your head and an impressive sculpture looms into sight. Come and get ready to be surprised and delighted by the beautiful beach city of Alicante.

Let's go to Alicante

We're going to take you on a tour of the historic heart of Alicante, starting with the iconic Santa Bárbara Castle. But be prepared to follow your instincts and stray off the path. If you're intrigued by what a little street or square has to offer, go and take a look. Alicante is made for exploring. For wandering. For enjoying. For discovering your own little gems and hidden corners.

Best things to do in Alicante

If you're looking for things to do on the Costa Blanca, the beautiful beach city of Alicante has attractions by the bucketload. Grand old buildings, traditional Spanish plazas, art galleries, museums, top shops, seafront restaurants, glorious beaches, a chic marina and sumptuous parks await you during your visit to Alicante.

We have to start our trip where Ali and Cantara fell in love, Santa Bárbara Castle. You can walk or drive up but the easiest way to get to Alicante castle is through the elevator in a tunnel in Avenida Juan Bautista Lafora, opposite Postiguet beach. There's a small fee for the elevator but admission to the castle is free, unless you do the 90-minute guided tour - which is a bargain at €5 and highly recommended.

Be warned, it is a steep walk through the castle grounds so wear flat shoes or trainers. If you're visiting in summer, it's best to go first thing in the morning or later in the evening. Thankfully there's a cafe within Alicante castle so you can sit, enjoy the views and refuel.

For around 1,000 years the castle has been guarding Alicante from its lofty position, 166 metres high on top of Monte Benacantil. You'll need a couple of hours to wander around and drink in those glorious, far-reaching views over the Mediterranean and the city's rooftops. Or you can take the guided tour lasting 90 minutes to hear the stories and adventures which have taken place here during its long and impressive history. Indeed this is one of Spain's most impressive medieval fortresses and one of the largest.

It dates back to the 9th century, when the Moors ruled the peninsula and you'll see this Arabic influence in the castle's architecture and layout.

Let your imagination run riot as you explore the dungeons, towers, palaces, squares, old church, parade ground and old cannons. Enjoy the most marvellous Mediterranean views from the very top next to the iconic tower which stars in many photos and Instagram posts. See if you can find where Ali and Cantara used to meet in her hidey-hole at the top of the castle.

Can you see the Moor's face engraved in Alicante castle?

You can appreciate how this magnificent fortress protected the city from its lofty mountain-top position until the 18th century. It has a long, varied history and even fell into foreign hands – including the English – a couple of times. It was also used as the city prison before falling into disrepair. Now the Santa Bárbara Castle in Alicante is an emblem of the city and a top tourist attraction.

Santa Bárbara Castle, Alicante, opening hours are: Winter (1 October to 31 March): 10.00 to 20.00h. April, May, June and September from 10.00 to 22.00. July and August from 10.00 to 24.00. Every day.

Within the castle is the MUSA museum (Museo de la Ciudad de Alicante or museum of Alicante city) where you can find out about the history of the city from prehistoric times. Open 10.00-20.00. Admission is €2.70, free for pensioners.

At the foot of the castle is the picturesque Parque La Ereta park, where you can have a rest in the shade. From here you can enjoy the most amazing city views during your stroll from the summit down to the heart of the city's historic quarter. You can also treat yourself to a meal with unique city views in La Ereta restaurant. The gastronomy is phenomenal where you'll taste the finest seasonal produce from Alicante with a modern twist.

If you're ready for a rest after exploring the castle and La Ereta park, head over the road to the sandy Postiguet beach. Around the beach are several cafés or take a stroll along the chic Alicante Port for even more restaurants and views of gorgeous yachts. At the far end of the port is the Museo Ocean Race museum, the starting point of four round-the-world yacht races as well as the next one in 2021.

It's time to explore Alicante's amazing city centre. First port of call is a favourite place for an ice-cream or cold drink - the lovely old Kiosko Peret kiosk on the Explanada de España, opposite the port. For a pick-me-up, ask for a blanco y negro (white and black) iced coffee. Or try the local drink, horchata, a refreshing vegan-friendly soft drink made from Valencian tiger nuts.

Now we're going to walk along the iconic Explanada de España in Alicante, arguably one of the most beautiful prom-enades in Spain. It's made up of thousands of little red, black and cream marble tiles designed to look like waves in the sea. They're so realistic, some people claim they feel seasick walking

The iconic tiles in Alicante's Explanada de España

across here! It's popular, day and night, with people enjoying a stroll or picking which restaurant they wish to dine in.

Keep walking along the Explanada with the sea to your left and you'll reach the beautiful little park, Parque de Canalejas. It has a wonderfully grand, old-fashioned air with its stone lion statues and gnarly old trees where, if you squint and use your imagination, you can envisage faces like the apple trees in the Wizard of Oz.

Heading back along the seafront to the port, it's time to visit the magnificent avenues and shops in Alicante. You'll find an eclectic mix of family-run shops, and high-street names as well as the famous El Corte Inglés department store.

Head up Avenida Doctor Gadea, a rather grand shopping street, leading to Plaza de los Luceros square with a super fountain in the centre. It's busy much of the time but a great area for hanging out or grabbing a cool beer at one of the bars. During the mid-summer hogueras fiesta (known as fogueres in valenciano) to celebrate San Juan and the longest day, this plaza is transformed. Imagine thousands of firecrackers called masclets being strung across the square and then set alight, reaching decibels of 120, 130 and more at lunchtime - 14.00. This is your introduction to the mascleta, a noisy, rhythmic pyrotechnic event typical of the Valencian region during fiestas. The sight, sound and smell are like nothing you'll ever experience. And it's probably about the only time the streets are crammed with people who are totally silent as they listen to the mascleta booming musically over their heads. During the hogueras fiesta, giant colourful statues are put up in the street and then burned on the night of San Juan, 24th June.

Turn into Avenida Alfonso El Sabio (Alfonso The Wise) to visit the impressive Modernist Mercado Central indoor market full of lush stalls selling fruit, vegetables, meat, fish and more. You can grab a meal here, look at the huge variety of seafood and buy sweet turrón – like nougat - made in the nearby town of Jijona (Xixona in valenciano).

Opposite the market, go down another impressive shopping street, Rambla Méndez Núñez, where you'll find the Museo de Fogueres museum telling you all about the history of this magical summer fiesta in Alicante. You can also see a few examples of the giant statues that go up in the streets a few days before San Juan, 24th June, and are then burnt to ashes on the night of San Juan.

Museo de Fogueres, Rambla Méndez Núñez, 29, is open: Tuesday to Friday 10.00-14.00 and 17.00-20.00. Saturday and Sunday 10.00-14.00. Closed Monday. Free entry.

You may by now have noticed that there seem to be just as many places to eat and drink in Alicante city centre as there are shops. You won't have to walk far for a drink, tapas, meal or ice-cream. A top place to try Alicante ice-cream is along the Rambla, the quaint Heladería Borgonesse, which has been making the most delicious ice-creams since 1984. This is next to Alicante's finest and most famous square, Plaza Portal de

Elche, built in the 19th century as a meeting point and water supply. It's still a super place to hang out and grab a coffee in the old-fashioned kiosk.

Remember to meander through the interconnecting streets such as the surreal Calle San Francisco, which looks like something straight out of a Disney movie or the Wizard of Oz with its yellow road, giant mushrooms, and snails. Again, it's crammed with restaurants and bars so is a rather quirky place to visit, day or night.

At the other end of Calle San Francisco is another fine square, Plaza Calvo Sotelo, with its own ornate kiosk to order a coffee or beer and watch the world go by.

As you've been wandering around, you'll have noticed a lot of public art in Alicante streets. It's wonderful to see sculptures and statues brightening the streets and bringing art to the people, don't you think? Among them are the lovely little statue of Icarus by Esperanza d'Ors with its tiny head and carrying a surfboard in the port, and the charming bronze statue El Adivinador (The Fortune Teller) by Juan Ripollés nearby next to the Plaza del Mar and Postiguet beach. As you wander, look out for traditional busts of famous people and impressive street art in Alicante including comic book characters, Marilyn Monroe and the poignant En Tu Memoria (In Your Memory) featuring a beautiful woman holding a candle near the Plaza de Toros.

So now you've had a stroll and, hopefully, a bite to eat, we need to tick off a few of the cultural things to do in Alicante, like museums and historic buildings. Don't forget to schedule in time for sunbathing on the beach in Alicante.

Many museums are in and around the town hall in the Plaza del Ayuntamiento, where we'll head first. Pop into the impressive Baroque ayuntamiento (town hall) with its barley sugar columns to see a little curiosity. Inside are several amazing rooms and the Cota Cero or Level 0 at the foot of the building's main staircase. This is the reference point from which Spain's cities are measured in metres above sea level.

Alicante City Council building, Plaza del Ayuntamiento, 1, is open: Monday to Friday 9.00-14.00. Closed weekends and fiesta days.

Plaza del Ayuntamiento is an exquisite square where they have an ice rink at Christmas and where one of the best statues is erected during hogueras in Alicante.

Just behind the town hall is the blue-domed 16th century

Concatedral de San Nicolás de Bari in Plaza del Abad Penalva. It's well worth a visit for its amazing chapel, considered to be one of the finest examples of Spanish Baroque, and elegant cloisters.

Concatedral de San Nicolás de Bari in Plaza del Abad Penalva is open: Tuesday to Friday 07.30-13.00 and 17.30-20.00; Saturdays, Sundays and public holidays 08.30-13.30 and 17.30-20.30. Closed Monday.

Heading towards Alicante castle, we come to MACA Museum of Contemporary Art in Alicante, opposite the Basílica de Santa María. Take a look at masterpieces by great avant-garde international artists without the crowds you'll get in a bigger city. As well as works by the likes of Joan Miró, Pablo Picasso, and Salvador Dalí, there's also an impressive collection of 500 works by Alicante artist Eusebio Sempere.

MACA, Plaza de Santa María, 3, is open: Tuesday to Saturday 10.00-20.00, Sunday and fiesta days 10.00-14.00. Closed Monday. Free entry.

Next stop, Basílica de Santa María, also in Plaza Santa María. Between the cathedral and the castle is Alicante's oldest church, the gorgeously Gothic Santa Maria basílica. Dating from the

14th century, it was built over the ruins of Alicante's oldest mosque - you'll find this happening a lot in Spain. It's well worth looking in to see the massive 16th century baptismal font and the Valencian Baroque organ of 1653.

Basílica de Santa María, Plaza Santa Maria, is open: Every day 10.00-13.00 and 18.00-19.30

Nearby is the Museo Bellas Artes Gravina fine arts museum housed in the 18th century Gravina Palace. It contains works of art from the Middle Ages through to the early 20th century.

MUBAG, Calle Gravina 13-15, is open: 1 September to June 30, Tuesday to Saturday from 10.00-20.00; Sunday and fiesta days from 10.00-14.00. From 1 July to 31 August, Tuesday to Saturday from 11.00-21.00; Sunday and fiesta days,11.00-15.00. Closed Mondays. Admission free.

Another little curiosity is the fascinating Museo de Aguas, Alicante museum of water, in Plaza del Arquitecto Miguel López. It's a three-minute walk from the basilica and you'll be rewarded with the best views over Alicante. You can also see a cave where water was stored during Medieval times and other cool displays.

Museo de Aguas, Plaza del Arquitecto Miguel López, is

open: September to May, Tuesday to Friday 10.00-14.00 and 17.00-20.00. Saturday and Sunday 10.00-14.00. June to August, Tuesday to Friday 10.00-14.00 and 18.00-21.00. Saturday and Sunday 10.00-14.00. Closed Monday. Free entry.

If you love Christmas then make sure you visit the Museo de Belenes showing many figures and scenes from the nativity.

Museo de Belenes, Calle San Agustin 3, is open: Monday to Friday from 10.30-13.30 and 16.45-19.45.

Around the other side of Alicante castle, heading north is the stunning MARQ Alicante Archaeological Museum, in Plaza Doctor Gómez Ulla. It has visiting exhibitions throughout the year but the permanent exhibition is an incredible journey through history. You can find out more about the Moors and their influence on Spain. Indeed, you'll get to know the history of Alicante from prehistoric times to today.

MARQ museum, Plaza Doctor Gómez Ulla, is open: June 16 to September 15, Tuesday to Saturday from 10.00-14.00 and 18.00-22.00. Sundays and fiesta days 10-00-14.00. Open from September 16 to June 15, Tuesday to Friday from 10.00-19.00. Saturday 10.00-20.30, Sundays and fiesta days 10.00-14.00. Closed Mondays. Small entry fee of €3 for adults.

After a wonderful time visiting Alicante museums, you may want to treat yourself to a spot of sunbathing at Postiguet beach or take a boat trip. A beautiful day out is to get the boat from Alicante port to the little island of Tabarca, a great spot for sunbathing, snorkelling or taking a peaceful walk. Tabarca is a protected Mediterranean Marine Reserve with crystal-clear waters which reminds many visitors of the Caribbean. It does get very busy in the height of the summer season but it's soothingly tranquil at other times of the year. Cruceros Kontiki has daily sailings to Tabarca and you'll find the boats midway along the port.

Yet another unusual attraction in Alicante is a visit to some of its 100 air-raid shelters to get a sense of how much Alicante suffered during the Spanish Civil War. Before that, we'll start just behind the central indoor market in Plaza 25 de mayo, named to commemorate the city's worst bombing of civilians. The tragedy occurred in 1938 when the market was packed with shoppers, mostly women and children. See the memorial dedicated to the 300 or so victims directly affected and the more than 2,000 people who were indirectly affected. Inside the market hall, the market clock is displayed in a special case with the time poignantly stopped at the hour of the bombing - 11.15.

If you walk towards the sea close to Avenida Dr Gadea, there's a small Spanish Civil War bunker in Plaza Balmis. Take a look at the doors shaped like submarine doors to protect the townsfolk against toxic gases released by chemical bombs. Cross over the Avenida to Plaza Séneca, where the old bus station used to be, to visit the shelter where around 1,200 citizens would seek refuge during an air raid. It's an eerie place to visit as you will hear recordings of the sound of the bombings, giving a rough idea of the horrors that people went through during the air-raids.

Plaza Séneca Civil War air-raid shelter is open: Tuesdays to Saturdays 10.00-14.00 and 16.00-20.00, and Sundays from 10.00-14.00. Closed Mondays

In this square, you will see two lovely large murals by the Alicante painter Gastón Castelló illustrating places of interest in his fine city.

Where to go out at night in Alicante

A great night out in Alicante is simply to wander the streets and pop into any bar or restaurant which takes your fancy. You can do a mini tapas and pub crawl by choosing different tapas to accompany your drink before moving on to as many bars as you wish. Otherwise, great entertainment in Alicante can be found at the following venues.

Teatro Principal de Alicante, Plaza Ruperto Chapi: Traditional old Neo-Classical theatre opened in 1847. Variety of shows from opera through to live music, drama and ballet.

Las Cigarreras Cultural Centre, Calle San Carlos 78: This old cigarette factory in Alicante employed thousands of workers in its 200-year history. Its warehouses have now been transformed into a top cultural centre with movies, live music and workshops among the many activities.

Freaks Arts Bar & Gallery, Calle Alona 8: Open every evening from Wednesdays to Sundays (19.00 throughout the year except in summer when it opens at 20.00). Popular with locals, to enjoy a drink or a meal while taking in art exhibitions, theatre shows, movies, workshops, and more.

Barrio de Santa Cruz: Alicante's old quarter with small white houses and old buildings whose balconies overflow with colourful flowers. Pop into any of the bars or restaurants for a cracking night out.

Alicante Port: Chic area full of lovely bars and restaurants. Great for alfresco dining or a cheeky pre-/post-dinner drink. Casino Mediterráneo Alicante is here too where you can play the slot machines and card games or visit the restaurants.

How to get to Alicante

Alicante airport at El Altet is just 14kms from the city centre. If you're hiring a car at Alicante airport, it's well signposted to the city. You can take the A70 and then the A31 or enjoy a more pleasurable route along the coast on the N332 to Alicante. Alicante Aerobus is the shuttle bus service which runs every 20 minutes, every day, 24 hours a day. Once in Alicante, you can hop on the bus or the tram to get around or explore further afield. But the city is compact and you can walk around many of the major attractions. If you're not planning to visit other Costa Blanca towns, then it's easier and more economical to use public transport as parking is expensive.

Best time to visit Alicante

Summer is the most popular time as it's hot and the beach is gorgeous. However, it is very crowded, flights are more expensive and it can be scorching hot. This is a fabulous desti-nation at any time of the year. You might want to book your visit to Alicante to coincide with the major fiestas.

Hogueras in Alicante, when they put the massive statues in the streets and let off the exceedingly loud mascletas, is held a few days before San Juan on 24th June while the burning of the statues occurs on the night of San Juan, and bonfire parties on the beach takes place on San Juan Eve, 23rd June.

Alicante at Easter is a very dramatic time with the brotherhoods holding various processions during Holy Week, when they carry magnificent, larger-than-life-size statues showing scenes from the main Easter events.

Christmas is rather magical because San Nicolás or Papá Noel (Santa Claus) lives in Alicante for much of the year. The Netherlands and Belgium celebrate the Fiesta of San Nicolas on 5th and 6th December. Every year Santa sets sail from Alicante in a steamboat to the Dutch coast to give presents and oranges to the children who have been good.

In Alicante you can visit Santa's grotto, see the amazing nativity scene set up in the Plaza del Ayuntamiento square and enjoy the special ice rink in this square too. Although the weather may not feel Christmassy to those of us from Northern Europe, America or Canada, the atmosphere is very special.

What's the weather like?

The summer months are very hot with an average high of 31° and a low of 21°. Often the temperatures will reach 38° or more. September can be a bit cooler. The autumn months of October and November are around the mid 20°s. It's also quieter and cheaper to visit Alicante out of high season, except during the UK school half-term holidays. Winter months of December to February are around 18° during the day and as low as 6° at night. Spring is a super time to visit, especially if you venture inland to see the beautiful blossom. Temperatures are still good with a high of 20° to 24° and a low of around 10°. Things can start heating up in June with a high of around 28° and the Spanish schools break up in this month so the beaches will get busy. There's very little rainfall although you might experience a gota fria (cold drop) of very intense rain and flooding lasting two or three days. This generally occurs in September or October.

Where and what to eat in Alicante

Paella, of course, is the number one dish but there are plenty of other rice dishes in Alicante. Paella Valenciana is the traditional paella with chicken, rabbit and snails. A favourite is Paella

Mixta with seafood and meat, usually chicken, so you can pick out your favourite bits. Fish lovers should try arroz a banda, rice cooked in fish stock. Otherwise order the catch of the day or any fresh fish. Also, try the local ice-creams and turrón - a type of nougat - from nearby Jijona.

There are great restaurants in Alicante so you'll certainly find ones which suit your palate and your pocket. Great ones to try are Dársena in Alicante Port, Monastrell on the other side of the Port, Nou Manolín in Calle Villegas, Capri in Calle San Ildefonso, Vivaldi Vermuteria in Calle Segura, and La Ereta which we mentioned before. A top restaurant for vegans or for plant-based meals is BodhiGreen in Calle San Fernando. Seriously though, the restaurants serve all types of cuisine from around the world so you won't go short of great places to eat out in Alicante.

Where to stay in Alicante

You'll find hotels in Alicante to suit all budgets and tastes from international chains to boutique hotels in historic buildings. Favourites are the Meliá for its location between Postiguet beach and Alicante port; Hotel Hospes Amérigo, Calle Rafael Altamira, in an old Dominican convent; Hotel La Milagrosa,

Calle Villavieja, for its fabulous views from the rooftop terrace; Hostal Smile & Co in Calle Rafael Terol is central, budget-friendly and pet-friendly; and AC Hotel Alicante, Avinguda d'Elx, for its rooftop bar and pool.

How long should I spend here?

You need a long weekend in Alicante at least to see the sights and to have some beach time. If you decide to spend longer, you'll be able to explore other nearby towns, such as taking a tour up the Costa Blanca coast or to take the complete tour in this book!

What to photograph that will look amazing on Instagram?

- Definitely a photo or a selfie at the top of the Santa Bárbara Castle near the turret.
- Get one of the amazing sunsets or sunrises.
- Find a tree with a really gnarly trunk that looks like a face or a cartoon.
- Your golden paella, of course.

Secret Alicante

Definitely walk past the big-name coffee shops and head for this absolute gem in the old town - Madness Coffee in Calle

San Nicolás with its lovely range of coffees and friendly staff.

Anyone with a sweet tooth will love visiting Panadería La Dulce Elsa bakers in Calle Segura. You'll find a delicious range of sweet and savoury artisanal products from the local area including the towns of Pinoso, Aspe, Cox and Busot. Try the bread from the nearby town of Mutxamel baked in a wood oven. This is a lovely place to stock up for a picnic or snacks for the beach.

If you fancy sightseeing but want to rest your feet after all the walking around you've done so far, you can hop on the tourist bus from March to November. Another lovely trip is to take the tram from Alicante to Benidorm. It only costs a few euros and is a beautiful, hour-long ride along the marvellous Costa Blanca coast.

Chapter 3: Who's the enchantress in Guardamar del Segura?

Remember that giddy feeling when you fall in love? How you are totally besotted with your new amour? How everything revolves around your new Mr or Mrs Right? You're totally wrapped up in each other. You can't eat. You can't sleep, except when you dream of your loved one. And, oh what dreams you have. Nothing else matters. You'd do anything for love. Love conquers all. You'll be together, forever.

Imagine then, how you'd feel if someone stepped in to crush your love and forbade you from ever meeting again.

Star-crossed lovers and unrequited love are the stuff that dramas are made of. This is another heartbreaking tale which took place right here in the Alicante province. We're heading to the Río Segura between Rojales and Guardamar to see how forbidden love can have far-reaching consequences.

On any ordinary day, the Río Segura looks pretty and peaceful. A few little boats bob up and down by the riverbanks. Birds sing prettily as they soar up in the blue skies. It's the perfect spot for a romantic walk or picnic. But venture here during San Juan and it's a totally different story.

Who knows what could happen if you're a handsome young male ripe for enticement by an endearing young woman.

Our tale begins in medieval times when the Moors ruled these Spanish lands. A coquettish and very lovely young Princess, Zulaida, lived here with her family as her father, the Moorish King, happened to rule these fertile lands. She was a lively young lady with her heart in the right place. But she was in love with the wrong man. For it was a handsome young Christian Prince who'd taken Zulaida's fancy. Let's read what happened.

"I cannot trust you," bellowed the King. His face glowed red like a volcano ready to erupt. "You cannot live here. You are banished from my Kingdom.

"Guards! Take this creature – for it is no daughter of mine – to Cabezo Soler, where she will live forever. And I mean forever."

Zulaida cried her prettiest tears that felt like the finest cut diamonds trickling down her pink cheeks. But even they failed to melt her father's cold heart. She had no tricks left to win round her father. The thought frightened her more than she could ever have imagined.

Zulaida screamed in fear as she tried to wriggle free from the soldiers who grabbed her. For she knew she would never survive in such a wild and desolate place. Remember, this was a pampered Princess who had people running around after her whenever she raised her dainty fingers. She had people to bathe her in fragrant oils. People to dress her. To cook for her. To undress her. She didn't have to do a thing except lift her little fingers to summon her servants who obeyed her every whim. She was so very bored and called her servants many times a day. She needed food, she would say. She needed water. What she really needed was company because she felt very lonely and craved friends to share her secrets and giggle with her.

So when she finally found her soulmate she was overjoyed. Now she had someone to whisper in her ear. Who adored her. Who laughed at the funny things she said. Luckily too, her beau was as noble as she. And the days flew by with this gorgeous, witty lover by her side.

Until now. Until her father caught wind of how serious the relationship was and stepped in.

"I hate you," she spat at her startled father. "I am in love with a Prince and you should be happy. This could be a happy union with a marriage between myself - a Princess — and my love. It would also be a happy union between us Moors and the Christians. Surely everyone can see it's advantageous for everyone concerned, even you Father Dearest."

Her wise words angered the King further. "Take her now before I really get angry," he bellowed. And at this, the guards marched her to the foot of Cabezo Soler, a bleak and desolate place next to the Río Segura, just outside Rojales on the way to Guardamar del Segura.

Her gallant Prince turned out not to be so honourable after all. He too enjoyed a very privileged life. It certainly didn't occur to him to follow the guards and save his loved one so they could live happily ever after. No, it was San Juan Eve and the self-centred little Prince wanted to have fun.

Zulaida was left to her own devices with no handsome beau riding to her rescue.

At first the Princess thought it is a cruel trick her father was playing on her. She truly believed he would send someone to fetch her back to the castle once he had calmed down.

Then night fell. She was surrounded by a black wall of silence. No-one called her name. No-one came for her. She was all alone for the first time in her life. Hungry. Scared. In the dark.

Zulaida slumped by a large tree and sobbed real tears this time. She cried herself to sleep and then had the weirdest dream. Or was it a warning?

She dreamt that a large black crow landed heavily on her left shoulder and cackled in her ear. "Aaawk, Aaawk. You're the talk of the town, my dear. You may not recognise me but I live in the rafters of your fine palace. Or should I say your former home. Aaawk, Aaawk.

"Everyone is talking about you and the curse your father has put on you. You'll never find anyone to break the curse. You're doomed to live here forever and ever and ever. Your father has left you to rot here although he has given you one very slender glimmer of hope. To lift the curse, you need to find a gallant young man to carry you to the river where you can wash your feet to remove the curse. But there is only one night of the year when you can lift the curse. And it just happens to be San Juan Night when every eligible young man is out enjoying the fiesta.

Aaawk! Aaawk! Aaawk!"

Zulaida woke up with a mighty shudder. She was still all alone and she feared the curse must be true.

Her belly rumbled. She hadn't eaten for 24 hours. But what could she eat?

The Princess was unable to fish. Did not know how to catch wildlife. And had little clue which plants to eat or which would kill her. She thought she would die. But she survived. Day after day after day. She really could live for all eternity unless she broke the curse. But how?

Every night Zulaida sobbed herself to sleep. But now her dreams were filled with schemes of how to lift this curse and exact revenge on her father. Unfortunately, she only had one opportunity a year in which to break the curse. If she failed, she had to wait another whole year in this wretched state before trying again. But that gave her plenty of time to think of how she would punish her father for what he had done to her.

For most people, the year passed very quickly. Zulaida never knew a year to drag so slowly and to be so very, very boring. But then San Juan arrived and she was ready.

Zulaida got up, combed her hair with twigs that she fashioned into a hairbrush and plaited her long, dark tresses as best she could. Remember she used to have servants do everything for her. Now she did everything for herself. Why, she'd even learned to cook!

As night fell, she heard footsteps and knew she must act.

Young Juan was wandering home alone after a joyous party celebrating the start of summer. The party was so fantastic it carried on all day. He had been out for 24 hours or more and was exceedingly tired. But he was young, carefree and was looking forward to spending the entire summer fishing with his brothers. Besides, he could hit his bed as soon as he got home, or so he thought.

It was a beautiful night with the stars twinkling brightly and the moon casting a shadowy light on the river. Juan stopped for a moment and watched the moon's reflection dancing in the ripples.

"Help me," a silvery, breathless voice called from behind a tree along the side of the road.

"How? Who are you? What do you want?" replied Juan.

Zulaida breathed more easily. Her bait was being reeled in.

"I need a brave, nay heroic, handsome young man to help me

break the spell that my heartless father put on me. Will you be my hero? Are you brave enough? Are you handsome enough?"

Juan puffed out his chest a little. Of course he was the right man for the job. Especially as his damsel in distress had such a pretty voice. And sounded a little flirtatious.

"I wonder how she'll reward me for saving her and breaking the curse," he thought to himself. "What do you need me to do?" he asked at once.

This wasn't the time to weigh up the pros and cons between helping this young lady or heading home to his comfy bed. This was a time for action.

"It's very simple," replied the silvery voice. "I'll be forever in your debt if you would just carry me over to the river where I can bathe my feet and wash off this stupid curse."

"Her voice sounds so delicate, I bet she's a dainty maiden and doesn't weigh much at all," thought the impetuous young man.

"No problem at all," replied her romantic hero, quite taken at the thought of seeing his maiden wash her pretty little feet in the river. "Here I come. Get ready to be rescued."

He swooped Zulaida up into his big strong arms and was

delighted to find she was as light as a peacock feather – and just as beautiful.

But, often when you think you're doing a simple favour for someone, it turns out it's never as easy as it first appears. Saving a cursed Princess is no exception.

As Juan strode confidently towards the river, Zulaida became heavier and heavier, and even heavier. Then, just as he was about to put her down by the riverbed, up popped a monstrous dragon (which could be a rather well-fed gecko who had eaten all the flies dancing on the surface of the water) and he was forced to turn heel and find another path.

Rio Segura at Guardamar del Segura. Looks peaceful, doesn't it?

This happened too many times to count. Juan wished he'd never heard the dulcet tones of the Princess or agreed to be her hero. Juan could not face another river monster. Nor could he hold on to her any longer as she now weighed as much as a small horse. He was so confused, so tired, and so scared of the monsters, that he didn't know which way led to the river any more.

His knees buckled and he fell to the ground, dropping Zulaida. The burden of breaking the mighty King's curse and being responsible for releasing the Princess was far too heavy for him to bear. He died. When the Princess realised her hero had failed her, she sobbed uncontrollably and crawled back to her hole in the mountain where she waited for another monotonous 365 days before trying to break the curse again.

Who knows how many families suffered because of Zulaida and her father's curse? How many families had their hearts broken because their gorgeous sons failed to come home on San Juan Night?

Come the next San Juan will her next victim be able to lift her curse? Well, it hasn't happened in the past 500 years. Maybe young men have got wind of the Legend of La Encantá –

the enchantress – as she is now called. Maybe now they avoid walking home alongside the river during San Juan. Who knows!

As we think of poor Zulaida and her victims it makes you wonder.

Parents are now keen to ground their children when they do something they disapprove of but should they be talking to them more, reasoning with them?

Was Zulaida really in love or was it just infatuation? If her father had left her alone would she have become tired of her Prince?

Is out of sight really out of mind?

Is 'banishing' things or people you disagree with the right way forward?

Could the Princess have won her father around by using reason rather than fake tears?

It's an interesting tale. No wonder the Legend of La Encantá has inspired many artists.

She stars in a novel by Fausto Cartagena, a play written by Salvador García Aguilar and directed by Alberto González Vergel and a short film called La Leyenda de la Encantá by Francisco Jorge Mora García and Joaquín Manuel Murcia

Meseguer produced in 2002. Composer Francisco Jorge Mora García has composed various pieces of music and songs inspired by her legend and San Juan.

You can also see an incredible re-enactment of the legendary La Encantá story to launch the start of the Moors and Christians fiesta every July. It is held in front of Guardamar Ayuntamiento and the stunning performance is an amazing spectacle of light, water and fire.

Now, in the following chapter, we shall go and visit Guardamar del Segura and Rojales to see how the Legend of La Encantá and other famous legends from this delightful region are remembered today.

Chapter 4: Get to know Guardamar and Rojales

Welcome to an amazing part of Costa Blanca South with fields cultivated with water from the Río Segura. Where sand dunes move to the rhythm of the wind and white mountains of salt astound visitors. It's also where you can see a very rare and extremely stunning pink lake.

Where to go in Guardamar del Segura and Rojales

There's only one place we can start this journey. By the Río Segura in Carrer del Malecón de La Encantá in Rojales. Here, next to the famous Carlos III bridge with its elegant three stone arches built in 1790 is a beautiful monument to La Encantada (La Encantá) with a handsome young man carrying a long-haired Zulaida alongside a monster. Close your eyes and listen. Can you hear La Encantá calling for help? Can you imagine being a young man alone during San Juan and being asked for help by this beautiful young woman? It's dark and suddenly you hear a voice whisper "Help me!". What would you do?

This is a lovely little town to visit to meet La Encantá and to see a little typical Spanish town, just inland from Guardamar del Segura, where we'll be visiting next.

La Encantá isn't the only legend of Rojales. In all, this small town on the Costa Blanca has five legendary tales and each one features in a gorgeous tiled mosaic in this very street, Carrer del Malecón de La Encantá. As well as La Encantá or Zulaida, the other oral traditions depicted in these mosaics are The Lost Child; the appearance of the Virgen del Rosario; The Child In The Well; and The Cross Of The Beata or Blessed Girl. They are a wonderful way for Rojales to show off its oral traditions and allow visitors to share these magical, historical stories.

Walk alongside the river a few metres from these stunning mosaics to find Rojales indoor market with a lovely selection of local produce, the town hall and the Capitol Rojales theatre, which is a lovely place to spend an evening in Rojales. You can

Carlos III bridge in Rojales

also see evidence of the Moorish influence on Rojales with a visit to the 16th century Azud Dam which diverts water from the Río Segura through a channel to irrigation ditches.

Tearing ourselves away from the river, let's visit the cave houses, Cuevas del Rodeo, south of the river and just a short walk over the Carlos III bridge. It's a haven for artists and a great place to pick up some local art or enjoy live music in its lovely little bar (remember to duck your head as it has a very low roof!). If you can, try to make your visit coincide with the monthly arts and crafts market. These are held on the first Saturday of the month during the summer from around 19.00 and then the first Sunday of the month starting at around 11.00 during the other months. Each month a different artist exhibits in the Sala Mengolero art gallery in one of the caves. As well as getting to know an unusual Costa Blanca attraction, you'll be rewarded with fabulous views over the area.

Returning to our Río Segura theme, head north of Rojales to the Museo de la Huerta or farming museum, in the former Don Florencio estate. Again, you will see the Moorish influence in the irrigation system, farming methods and distribution of water from the river.

Let's travel 11kms to the coastal town of Guardamar del Segura. On the way we pass the Cabezo Soler site where the unfortunate Zulaida is forced to live forever and ever.

Guardamar, meaning guardian of the sea, has glorious beaches with a scented backdrop of pine forests and dunes adding to the beauty of this stretch of the Costa Blanca coast. For peace and quiet, take a stroll through the Alfonso XIII forest, 800 hectares of sand dunes and trees including pines, palm trees and eucalyptus. This was built by engineer Francisco Mira I Botella as a natural wall to protect the town and its precious salt lakes from the shifting sands. Now, there are more than 600,000 trees protecting the town and providing a lovely scented backdrop for beach-goers.

Guardamar is a firm favourite with families because of its 11kms of fine, sandy beaches. Popular beaches include the Babilonia beach with its beautiful beach-front fishermen's cottages decorated with colourful, ornate tiles. Unfortunately erosion has taken its toll over recent years. You may want to find a spot on the sandy Playa Centro, town centre beach at the southern end of the dunes near Parque Reina Sofía park or Playa Els Tossals, near the dunes.

Definitely take a stroll or picnic in Guardamar's Reina Sofía park as it's a wonderful oasis. Keep an eye out for the animals who've made this their home including red squirrels, ducks, peacocks and turtles. On summer evenings, music and entertainment are held in this gorgeous park and each year the Nits d'Estiu (Summer Nights) concert allows visitors to enjoy music in a very magical setting.

Just behind the park on a hill stands Guardamar castle. Founded in 1271, this was actually a walled village with a castle at the highest point. Not much of it remains but it's worth walking up for lovely views over Guardamar.

Afterwards, return to Guardamar to visit the MAG archaeological museum. You'll find out more about Guardamar's 2.5-million-year history including the time when it was all under the sea and the arrival of the Moors.

MAG (Museo Arqueológico de Guardamar) Calle Colón 60, is open: Tuesday to Saturday from 11.00-14.30 and 17.30-20.30.

To find out more about the forestry engineer Francisco Mira I Botella, who began the reforestation of the Guardamar dunes in 1896 and dedicated 28 years of his life to this work, you can visit the museum in his former home. However, at the time of publication, restoration works were being carried out to improve Guardamar castle and the Casa Museo Ingeniero Mira.

Casa Museo Ingeniero Mira, Plaça de la Constitució 7, is open: Mondays to Saturdays, 10.00-15.00.

You simply cannot come to this area without visiting the amazing pink lake of Torrevieja. There are two salt lakes or salinas here – one pink and one blue-green. The pink one is incredible. It contains pigments of the Halobacterium bacteria which lives in extreme salty environments such as this lake and also in the Dead Sea in Asia and the Great Salt Lake in Utah, USA. That and an algae called Dunaliella Salina are what make it this amazing colour. Shrimps living in the lake and feeding on the bacteria are also pink. In turn, the flamingos eat the shrimp and also turn a lovely shade of pink.

From Guardamar to the Torrevieja salinas or lakes, it is a 30-minute drive south along the N332. A far more fun way to explore these salt lakes is to go into Torrevieja city centre and take the special tourist train. You'll go past the mountains of salt which can be 20 metres high (about the same as a 7-storey building) and find out more about these amazing lakes which produce around 700,000 tonnes of salt each year.

The trip takes about one hour and starts in the Paseo de la Libertad in Torrevieja at 10.00, 11.00, 12.00, 13.00, 14.00, 16.00, 17.00, 18.00, 19.00h and 20.00.

How to get to Rojales and Guardamar del Segura

Rojales is about a 35-minute drive from Alicante airport along the AP7. Get off at exit 740 and continue on the CV91 and the CV860 to Rojales. To Guardamar from Rojales takes about 15 minutes. Get back on the CV91 or the CV920 east. Get on the N332 towards Guardamar. The Costa Azul bus links Rojales and Guardamar and goes to Alicante city and Torrevieja.

What's the weather like?

This area enjoys around 320 days of sunshine and very little rainfall. It is typical Costa Blanca weather which means it's very hot in July and August - it can reach the high 30°s - and still mild in the winter months with an average high temperature of around 18° in December and January.

Best time to visit Guardamar and Rojales

Lovely times to visit these areas are for the Moors and Christians fiesta in Guardamar del Segura in mid-July and the hogueras de San Juan fiesta on and around San Juan on June 23 and 24. Rojales Moors and Christians is held in mid-June.

In July and August, the Costa Blanca beach resorts are super crowded, so unless you're planning to spend a lot of time on the beach, these months are best avoided. A wonderful time to visit is during winter or around Christmas as the weather is still lovely and warm – perfect for exploring the fascinating attractions in Guardamar del Segura and Rojales.

What type of place is it?

Rojales and Guardamar are definitely on the tourist map. They're only around 30 minutes from Alicante airport and surrounded by golf courses and the best beaches on the Costa Blanca South. You'll find many English-speaking people around but these towns still have a very Spanish flavour.

Where and what to eat in Guardamar del Segura and Rojales

Guardamar is where the small, sweet ñora red peppers are cultivated. These are dried and used generously in countless dishes from stews to sauces. Being by the sea, fresh fish and shellfish are widely used, either in rice dishes such as paella or simply grilled or fried. The Guardamar fishing fleet will bring in the freshest fish from the bay, including sea bream and sea bass along with exquisite seafood, especially the local prawns.

Every June Guardamar holds the delicious Setmana Gastronòmica de la Nyora i el Llagostí ((Gastronomic Week of the ñora and prawn) gastronomy fiesta with the symbol of Guardamar - the ñora pepper - and the local shellfish taking pride of place.

You'll be spoilt for choice for great Guardamar restaurants but they include Restaurante Le Bleu, Carrer Azorín 22, a very stylish restaurant serving superb Mediterranean food. The tasting menu is very popular and a great price for the quality of the food at around €30.

Restaurante Jaime in Guardamar del Segura is close to the Reina Sofía park and the beach. Its location and great seafood make it a popular choice for locals. For local Valencian dishes, go to Valenti Playa in Avenida Europa or Restaurante Rodero in the same street.

Restaurante La Perla Roja, Calle Zeus 4, on the edge of La Marquesa Golf Course, near Rojales, is a firm favourite as it has a lovely interior and a fixed-price Mediterranean menu.

In Rojales itself, a super place to get fine food with local fresh ingredients is Restaurante Casa Paco in Partida lo Garriga 42. The fixed-price menus are great value or just choose a plate of the day, which changes daily but you'll often find paella among the choices. It has a super variety of Mediterranean dishes, barbecued meats and home-made desserts.

Where to stay

For location alone, the 4-star Parque Mar hotel in Carrer Gabriel Miró, Guardamar, is surrounded by pine trees and great value.

Hotel Meridional, Av. de la Llibertat 64, has sublime sea views and a lovely gourmet restaurant, El Jardin, offering the best Mediterranean cooking with sea views too.

Hotel La Laguna Spa & Golf is a 4* resort just 15 minutes by car from Guardamar beaches and near to the Lagunas de la Mata nature reserve.

Hotel La Finca Golf & Spa Resort has superb spa facilities and for sports lovers, there is golf, tennis, paddle courts and a fitness centre. The restaurant serves gorgeous Mediterranean food and there's even a nightclub on the premises, the Suite Lounge Club. This resort is for adults only.

If you like livelier resorts, then you'll find plenty of apartments and hotels in Torrevieja to suit all budgets. There's also a wide range of restaurants and shops including one of the biggest open-air markets in Spain held every Friday morning.

How long should I spend here?

We'd recommend a couple of days in Rojales and Guardamar as this gives you some free time for the beach plus a chance for a proper look around each of the towns. Don't forget to stop off at the Torrevieja and La Mata lagoons.

What to photograph that will look amazing on Instagram?

- Definitely get a photo of the pink lake – at times it's almost red. Many people do not realise that there is a pink lake on the Costa Blanca, so your photo will definitely get talked about on social media.

- Also get a picture of the salt mountains.

- If you go into Torrevieja to catch the tourist train around the salt lakes, get a picture taken with the Bella Lola statue at Paseo Marítimo Juan Aparicio. It's a melancholy statue of the lovely Lola looking out to sea and hoping for her fisherman husband to return home. He never does!

Secret Rojales

One of the best kept secrets (until now) is the amazing La Casa de Las Conchas (the house of shells) in Calle Rodeo near the cave houses in Rojales. It is spectacular, seriously. Over many years, the then owner Manuel Fulleda Alcaraz decorated his house with shells - another image to amaze your social media followers!

Chapter 5: How Armengola saved Orihuela from massacre

Orihuela would be totally different today if it hadn't been for the bravery of the legendary Armengola. In the 13th century, when she lived in Orihuela, it was a frontier city ruled by the Moors under the Muslim governor Benzaddon. The castle was a powerhouse, a fortress, to keep the city safe from pirates and marauders. The places of worship were mosques. And Orihuela was known as Uryala.

Today the castle is in ruins but 700 or so years ago it was one of the grandest castles in all of Spain. Now it stands as a reminder of Orihuela's impressive city with a unique history. Take a look up at the castle and picture Armengola walking up there each day to work for the governor. Imagine how she must have felt when she realised her kinsfolk were under threat by the very man who employed her and whose son she adored as if he were her very own flesh and blood. Can you imagine how difficult it was for her to risk her own life to save her town?

Stand in Orihuela, touch its city walls and feel the colossal history surrounding you. You're about to hear one small but very significant chapter of the city's history – The Legend Of Armengola.

Hermenegilda Eugenia, wife of the herbalist Pedro Armengol, loved her job as it basically involved playing all day with her young charge, Benzaddon's son, within the castle walls. She realised, as a Christian, she was honoured to be given this important role looking after the son of the most powerful man in Uryala. But she loved it. She loved the way his deep brown eyes widened as she told him stories of legendary heroes, gods and kings. She loved the way he shrieked excitedly as they played hide and seek throughout the vast castle. She loved meal-times when they shared exotic rice dishes and sweet almond desserts.

All in all, life was fantastic. Even though they had their religious differences, the Muslims and Christians rubbed along just fine. Armengola was treated well by the governor who valued her affection and fierce loyalty to his treasured first-born son.

Benzaddon trusted her implicitly. He secretly watched her as she played with his beloved son in the castle gardens, singing songs and sharing picnics of sweet dates and dainty almond cakes. He knew she couldn't love his little boy any more. And his son loved her too, like a mother. Nay, more than a mother because Armengola spent more time with the boy than his wife ever did. She was always too busy chatting with her sisters, braiding her hair or changing the menu after the cooks had been to the market to get all the ingredients. Obviously, these were all far more important things than taking care of a child and making sure he was raised to be respectful to everyone. Benzaddon raised his eyes to the skies and thanked heaven for Armengola.

But all of this was about to come crashing down. Their delightful lives were about to be shattered.

One morning, as usual, Armengola headed up the steep, winding hill to the castle. Usually, she practically skipped up to the top because she was so keen to get to work. On this particular day, she trudged slowly as if her feet were made of the heaviest lead. Her heart felt just as heavy.

"I hope it's just a horrid rumour," she sighed to herself. "Everything is OK, here. We have our differences but we get along just fine. Now people are going to be killed. Many, many people." Armengola sighed again as tears as big as pearls fell down her ashen cheeks.

Her tears fell faster at the thought of losing many of her dear friends. Why should people go to war because of religion? It didn't make sense to the sensitive young woman. She loved her husband Pedro with all her heart. They were both Christians and had so much in common. They loved to dance and play music. Armengola also loved her young charge, who was Muslim. She saw no reason why they couldn't continue to live together as they had been doing for the past oh-so many years.

Her mind flashed back to the previous evening's events when she was preparing a simple supper of fish and rice. Her husband had rushed in from work, pecked her on the cheek and breathlessly whispered in her ear: "You'll never guess what my patients have been telling me."

Without waiting for her reply, he continued: "They say the King's troops are within a day's ride of here. They say they are going to storm the castle walls and take back Uryala. We'll be a Christian city again. They say they have hundreds, maybe 1,000 troops, coming to save us."

"Save us from what?" thought Armengola to herself as she turned around to dish up supper. "Save us from a life of peace and harmony? Why do we need saving? Why do things have to change and is change necessarily a good thing?"

Armengola remembered the stories her parents and grandparents told her about the riches that the Moors brought to Uryala.

"We have them to thank for the orchards full of the sweetest oranges, lemons, olives and almonds. They bought irrigation to keep the water flowing through the orchards to provide a rich harvest of fruit. They introduced rice and golden saffron to create the most delicious paellas. And they built the magnificent castles to guard the city from pirates, robbers and marauders," she thought to herself.

The Moors and the Christians had been living together and learning from one another for hundreds of years. Her husband learned to use different herbs – brought to Spain by the Arabs – to cure and treat his community.

"What's so different between a Christian and a Muslim? We all want to live the best life possible. To love and look after our family and to enjoy life in Uryala," thought Armengola wisely before turning in for the night.

The following morning, she hated the thought of working. Of facing Benzaddon, knowing what she did. Knowing that troops were reported to be on their way to kill him.

"What will happen to the boy?" she wondered. Her blood ran as cold as the ice on the nearby Sierra Helada at winter when she realised what his fate would be. She shook her head free from such tragic thoughts when she reached the castle.

As she was allowed through the enormous brass door and into the castle, she felt something was wrong. There was a tension, mixed with excitement in the air. Her heart skipped a beat. And then another.

"What if they've heard the rumours of an invasion? What if they ask me if I know anything," she wondered. But Armengola needn't have worried about that. Yes, Benzaddon had heard talk about the Christian army. But he had a cunning plan of his own, which was far worse.

As Armengola entered the governor's private quarters and headed towards the nursery, she heard the governor talking to his four most-trusted soldiers. "Forewarned is forearmed. We'll jump the gun and kill them first.

"We'll act today, at midnight. We'll head into the city. The Christians will be relaxed because tomorrow is a fiesta for them. They have the day off, they'll eat well and drink wine. A lot of wine. And they believe that King Jaime's army is on its way to save them. They won't suspect us at all.

"We'll move in small groups with every sword and knife we possess and slay the lot of them. By the time their precious King arrives, there will be no-one left to greet him and no-one for him to liberate." With that parting shot, the governor threw back his head and roared with laughter. To Armengola's ears, it sounded manic. To the soldiers, it was pure genius.

Armengola froze. "How can he laugh at such a callous plot. The streets will be filled with people – men, women and children – on such a balmy evening. And they're all going to die," she pondered.

There was only one thing for it. Armengola prayed harder than she had ever prayed in all her life. She prayed to the Saints Justa and Rufina, whose feast day they were celebrating in the morning. All being well.

"Saint Justa and Saint Rufina, I beseech you to protect our city and help your faithful Christians...."

Her prayers were stopped short. Benzaddon was calling her name.

"Armengola, you have been a loyal and faithful servant to me and my son, for which I thank you. As a token of my gratitude, I command you to go home, find your daughters and leave the city."

He handed the bewildered woman a document with his official seal allowing her free passage from the city of her birth. He was sparing her life and those of her daughters. But was life worth living without her husband, her friends, her beloved city?

She turned and left without saying a final farewell to her young charge, as she wanted to get out of the castle before the governor changed his mind.

She ran down the hill into the city. But instead of turning right towards her home to collect her daughters, she took a left turn towards the secret meeting-place of some Christian rebels and told them of the cruel governor's wicked plan.

Upon which, they drew up a counterplan of their own.

As night began to fall, Armengola was seen walking up the windy path towards the castle. It looked as though she was accompanied by her two daughters, going to thank Benzaddon for his enormous generosity towards them in sparing them.

Only her accomplices were not her lovely daughters. By her side were Arum and Ruidoms, two brave soldiers disguised as young maidens but armed with swords. Together they strode purposefully towards the castle. Helpfully, their path was lit by two bright stars believed to be the Saints Justa and Rufina whom Armengola had called upon a few hours earlier.

Close behind this brave trio, every Christian man in Uryala traced their steps. Luckily the saints did not light up their way and they were well hidden. Armengola and her 'daughters' approached the main gate when a strong voice called out: "Halt! Who goes there?"

"It is I, Armengola, and my daughters. We want to thank our beloved governor for his kindness before we leave."

The gate creaked open and Armengola's accomplices quickly drew their swords, rushed in and slayed the guards. With a mighty roar that rumbled throughout the Kingdom, their fellow Christians poured through the castle gate.

It was a terrible night. So many deaths. So much destruction. But what else could they have done to save themselves and their city?

By the time King Jaime I and his army reached Uryala, the fighting was over and the Christians had already reclaimed their beloved city, thanks to the heroic Armengola who put her city and its people before herself. Now they were liberated and could really celebrate their saints' day with gusto. They feasted like never before. They sung like a caged canary tasting freedom for the first time. They ate the finest foods from the castle kitchens and raided the cellars to enjoy the sweetest wines produced from their fertile lands.

At the head of the celebrations was Armengola. She is

Armengola takes centre stage in this ornate fountain in Orihuela forever remembered and honoured for her amazing, selfless act which saved Uryala.

More than 750 years later, Armengola still takes pride of place in the city's Moors and Christians fiestas celebrating the day the Christians recaptured Orihuela on the 17th July, 1242. Without her, Orihuela, as it is known today, would have a completely different history. So it is only right that Armengola, legendary heroine of the Reconquista, is a treasured icon here.

Every summer, Orihuela hosts a massive celebration in honour of the Reconquista of Orihuela and their Saints Justa and Rufina. In memory of how the saints guided Armengola and her two soldiers to the castle to overthrow the Moors, two decorative lights are placed over the castle during the Moors and Christians fiesta.

And each year, one proud woman is chosen to represent Armengola during the festivities. She is handed the precious Toisón, which is Armengola's decorated necklace or chain, at a special celebration in the Teatro Circo in Orihuela.

If you visit Orihuela during its Moors and Christians fiesta, held on and around 17th July, you can witness a dramatic production of the Reconquest of the castle to see how Armengola saved her city. It was written by Orihuela playwright Atansio Die Marin and Orihuela poet Joaquin Mas Nieves.

As we think about Armengola, has life changed so very much? Would people put themselves in danger and rush in to save their home town or expect someone else to do it today?

How many people would settle for a peaceful life, even if it means living under siege, rather than stand up and fight for what's rightfully their own?

Do we take positive action enough today or do we:

a) say there's nothing we can do and do nothing?

b) wait for someone else to take the lead and act first?

Do we take risks today, like Armengola did, or are we more passive for fear of repercussions?

Let's go and visit the legendary Armengola's birthplace and see just how important she is to this fine city.

Chapter 6: Unique attractions in Orihuela

How exciting to be visiting the city saved by Armengola. To walk in her footsteps and envisage how this ordinary woman must have felt knowing her employer was plotting to destroy her family, her friends, her home. You're going to see our heroine for the very first time.

Let's go to Orihuela

Firstly, let's visit the places in Orihuela which played their part in this fantastic legend. We're going to see how important Armengola is to this fine city and why her name will always be remembered.

A lovely place to start is the suburb where Armengola and her fellow Christians lived and where there is now a street called Calle la Armengola, named in honour of Orihuela's most famous heroine. It's a pretty anonymous street but look up the castle. Imagine the steep walk to the castle which Armengola trod every day.

Close your eyes and picture how Orihuela would have looked in Armengola's time.

You will also see a striking monument to our heroine in this suburb with text written by Mossen Jaume Ferrer.

Now let's head to two very important landmarks in Calle Francisco Die to see with our own eyes the lovely way that Armengola is revered and commemorated. Take a look at the eye-catching, ornate tiled Pozos de Cremós fountain with its gorgeous illustration and a portrait of the lovely heroine in pride of place. Wow, have they done Armengola proud.

Let's go to the very beautiful seat of the Association of Moors and Christians St Justa and Rufina, called the Casa Del Festero, and the Museo de la Reconquista (Reconquista museum). Remember, Justa and Rufina lit the way when Armengola and two soldiers disguised as her daughters headed up to the castle to save their city.

Get reacquainted with the legend herself inside the Reconquista museum where you can see Armengola's special necklace called the Toisón, an exhibition of costumes and a portrait of Armengola by Vicente Navarra. Seeing these amazing exhibits brings to life this powerful story of how one incredible woman saved her city.

Museo de la Reconquista museum is open: Tuesdays

to Saturdays from 10.00-14.00 and 16.00-19.00. Sundays and fiesta days from 10.00-14.00. From June 1 to September 30, the afternoon opening hours are from 17.00-20.00. Free entry.

When you look up to the castle, you'll begin to realise just how formidable Armengola's task was. Today, the castle is in ruins but from its lofty heights 240 metres atop of the Sierra de Orihuela mountain, you get a sense of how this fortress dominated the skyline from its excellent defensive position. You can walk to the top but it's an almighty scramble although you'll be rewarded with great, far-reaching views over Orihuela and nearby mountains. For many of us, our imagination is sufficient to breathe in the atmosphere of that dark, dreadful night when Armengola freed her city from the grip of the Moors.

You'll get an amazing impression of how Orihuela looked in Armengola's day at the Museo de la Muralla (museum of the wall). It's a four-minute walk past the glorious Ayuntamiento de Orihuela, the town hall, towards the river to the Museo de la Muralla, in the basement of the building Casa del Paso. Walking through the corridors, you'll feel yourself stepping back in time and really understand the importance of Orihuela throughout the ages. Here are the preserved walls and towers from the Almohad period, Arab baths, Islamic streets and houses and a Gothic palace. There's an image of medieval Orihuela in the exhibition so you can envisage how the city looked during Armengola's time.

Now, we'll bid Armengola farewell because this incredible tale of courage isn't Orihuela's only claim to fame. It has plenty more fascinating facts which make this city unique.

Let's meet Orihuela's devil and discover its impressive Holy Week parades. Get ready to be amazed as we find out more about Easter in Orihuela while visiting the fabulous historic heart of this city, full of drama, theatre, architecture and art.

There's nowhere better to start than in the Museo de la Semana Santa (Holy Week Museum) in Plaza de la Merced, which is built on the site of the old Nuestra Señora de la Merced (Our Lady of Mercy) church, which still retains its 16th century Renaissance facade.

Holy Week in Orihuela has been declared of International Touristic Interest for its emotional processions along the old, narrow city streets. This is where passion and art combine to dramatise Easter scenes from the Last Supper to the Resurrection. These powerful Orihuela Easter processions awaken all the senses. The scent of incense, the beating drum, the eerie silence of the Holy Thursday procession. The exquisite larger-than-life-size statues depicting the Last Supper, the Way Of The Cross, the Crucifixion and other famous Holy Week events. Easter in Orihuela is an incredibly special time. You'll get an amazing sense of this as you step through the doors of the Semana Santa museum and see these marvellous statues up close. You will see works by famous Spanish artists and sculptors such as Francisco Salzillo and Nicolás de Bussy as well as other sacred art dating from the 14th century.

El Museo de Semana Santa, Plaza de la Merced 1, is open: Tuesdays to Saturdays from 10.00-14.00 and 16.00-19.00. Sundays from 10.00-14.00. From June 1 to September 30 the afternoon opening times are from 17.00-20.00.

Let's take a lovely stroll along the Río Segura to our next stop, the stunning Orihuela Cathedral, Santa Iglesia Catedral del Salvador y Santa María. Remember we visited the Segura river in Chapter 3 when we met the enchantress, Zulaida.

The formidable Gothic Orihuela Cathedral of El Salvador and Santa Maria, dating from the 13th century, is a cultural heritage site. It's one of Spain's smallest cathedrals and, like many other cathedrals and churches in Spain, it is built on the site of a former mosque. Stop to marvel at its wonderful bell tower before stepping inside for impressive Renaissance works of art and a rather grand 18th century Baroque organ. Don't miss the Museum of Sacred Art, in the 16th century Episcopal Palace, where you can see Diego Velázquez's Temptation of St Thomas Aquinas painting and more works by the sculptor Francisco Salzillo from Murcia.

Orihuela cathedral in Calle Ramon y Cajal is open: Tuesdays to Fridays from 10.30-14.00 and 16.00-18.30, and from 10.30-14.00 on Saturdays. From June 1 to September 30, the afternoon opening hours change to 17.00-18.30. Admission €2.

The Episcopal Palace and Museum of Sacred Art next door opens: Tuesdays to Saturdays from 10.00-14.00 and 16.00-19.00, and from 10.00-14.00 on Sundays and feast days. From June 1 to September 30, the afternoon opening hours change to 17.00-20.00. Admission €4.

It's just a four-minute stroll from here to the Iglesia Santas Justa y Rufina church in Calle Santa Justa, honouring the city's patron saints. Look up at the beautiful Gothic church tower which marks another claim to fame for Orihuela. The tower houses the oldest clock in the Valencia Comunidad, installed in 1439. In the corners of the tower, you'll see fabulous gargoyles and fantastic animals.

Iglesia Santas Justa y Rufina in Calle Santa Justa is open: Tuesday, Wednesday and Friday from 10.00-13.45 and 16.00-18.00; Thursdays from 11.00-13.45 and 16.00-18.00; and Saturdays from 10.00-13.45. Volunteers look after the church so you may find some changes to the opening times. Entry is free.

In many ways we've saved the best to last. Now it's time to meet the unique devil, which is both male and female – Nicolás de Bussy's Diablesa housed in the 18th century San Juan de Dios archaeological museum. Get ready to be awe-struck.

This winged devil with horns and breasts is the only demon of its kind allowed to take part in the Easter processions in Spain. During the Easter Saturday procession, the Diablesa is refused entry to Orihuela Cathedral because you can't let the Devil into church, can you?

San Juan de Dios museum, Calle Hospital, is open: Tuesdays to Saturdays from 10.00-14.00 and 16.00-19.00

Nicolás de Bussy's Diablesa in Orihuela

pm; 10.00-14.00 on Sundays and fiesta days. From June 1 to September 30, the afternoon opening hours change to 17.00-20.00. Free admission.

Wait, there's more! Orihuela has yet another claim to fame. The poet Miguel Hernández was born in Calle San Juan in Orihuela on 30th October, 1910. He died of tuberculosis in 1942 while imprisoned for his active support of the Republicans during the Spanish Civil War. The sufferings and misery caused by war and hate are reflected in his poetry. One of his best-known works is the poignant Nanas de la cebolla (onion lullaby) written for his son after his wife sent him a letter in prison saying the family were living on bread and onions. The Miguel Hernández museum, dedicated to this great Spanish literary figure, is inside the house where Miguel and his family lived from 1914 to 1934. Step inside to find out how a typical family from Orihuela lived at the beginning of the 20th century

Casa-Museo Miguel Hernández, Calle Miguel Hernández, is open: Tuesdays to Saturdays 10.00-14.00 and 16.00-19.00; Sundays and fiesta days from 10.00-14.00. From June 1 to September 30, the afternoon hours change to 17.00-20.00. Free entry.

For our final stop, let's head back to the district where Armengola lived to visit the impressive Murales de San Isidro. This open-air museum of murals is a loving tribute to Miguel Hernández and to freedom. In May 1976 several artists, writers and musicians gathered in Orihuela as part of the movement, Tribute From The People Of Spain to Miguel Hernández (Homenaje de los pueblos de España a Miguel Hernández).

Remember, these were difficult times for Spain as Franco had just died and the country was emerging from a long and brutal dictatorship towards democracy and liberty. This Orihuela suburb became a hub for artists to show solidarity and unity.

In 2012, on the 70th anniversary of the poet's death, the town hall and local artists restored some of these original murals and, every March, new ones are added. It creates a stunning and colourful cascade of creativity running along these hillside streets. It is a beautiful place to end our journey. We started with Armengola, who fought for the freedom of her people and Orihuela, and ends with Miguel Hernández who also fought for freedom. Both their names and their beliefs will live on forever in this wondrous city.

How to get to Orihuela

It's about a 40-minute drive from Alicante airport to Orihuela. The fastest route is via the AP7 and A7. Take exit 545 from the AP7 and turn left on to the CV930 into Orihuela. A much more scenic route, which only adds about 15 minutes to your journey, is to drive along the N332 along the coast to Guardamar del Segura, which we visited in Chapters 3 and 4. At Guardamar get on the CV91 to Orihuela.

The train from Alicante to Orihuela takes just under an hour. There are buses from Alicante city and airport to Orihuela with the fastest bus taking around an hour while the slow buses take nearly two hours, the bonus being you will get to see a bit of the Spanish countryside during your journey.

What's the weather like?

Like the rest of the Alicante province, Orihuela has a temperate climate. The hottest months are July and August with a maximum temperature of 32° or more. November to April, the maximum temperature is from 16° to 20° which is ideal for exploring, although you'll need a sweater or jacket for the evenings when temperatures can fall to 5°.

Best time to visit Orihuela

Obviously the very best times to go to Orihuela are during the Moors and Christians fiesta held in and around July 17, the day that Armengola saved the city, and during Holy Week. The city will be packed during these fiestas so it's best avoided if you don't like noisy, crowded places with festivities going on all through the night and starting again early in the morning. Spring and autumn are beautiful times to visit Orihuela as the weather is still very good but pleasant for wandering around and sightseeing. Visit in the summer months if you're planning a beach holiday on the Orihuela Costa.

What type of place is it?

Many tourists head for the gorgeous beaches on the Orihuela Costa or Torrevieja and stay there. Orihuela is typically Spanish. It has that buzzy Spanish feel about it. There will be other tourists but mostly from other Spanish areas.

Where and what to eat in Orihuela

Paella and rice dishes, such as arroz a banda, will be plentiful in Orihuela restaurants. There is also a good selection of tapas bars where you can try tasty snacks such as prawns, jamon, Russian salad or meatballs. In the Ociopia shopping centre in Orihuela is 100 Montaditos, a national chain serving montaditos - snacks usually served on slices of bread.

A pretty place to eat is Las Huellas de Miguel Hernández in Pasaje Canto de la Pasion. The dishes are based on local produce but with an artistic twist. They even look like works of art on a plate! Try the dish called Nanas De La Cebolla, named in honour of Miguel Hernández's famous poem.

The Agus Gastrobar in Calle Valencia is extremely popular and has great-priced lunchtime menus (menu del dia).

Where to stay in Orihuela

It's a small city so there aren't too many hotels. In the heart of the city is the gorgeous historic Palacio de Tudemir. This former palace, dating back to 1755, still retains its original character and elegance. Plus it has a car park. Another lovely central hotel is the Hostal Rey Teodomiro in Avenida Teodomiro. There is a much greater selection of hotels along the Orihuela Costa and Torrevieja, less than 30kms from Orihuela city.

How long should I spend here?

You can easily see the main sights in a weekend but spend longer if you want time on the beach or to visit the neighbouring towns such as Elche - city of 200,000 palm trees and shoe factory outlets - Alicante or Murcia.

What to photograph that will look amazing on Instagram

- Head to the little Plaza Nueva square, just south of the river, for its rather ornate Modernist lantern. It reminds us of the decorative wrought-iron features in the famous Paseo de Gracia in Barcelona. There's seating around the base so you should get a grand selfie and then let people guess where you are. See how many say Barcelona!

- Anywhere by the Río Segura and its fine bridges will make beautiful photos, particularly at sunrise or sunset.

Secret Orihuela

We're going underground in Orihuela to visit the Santa Justa Civil War bomb shelter. It starts by the old police station and goes under the rock beneath the neighbourhood of Triana to end in Calle Maestro Esteban. You need to book a visit by calling 0034 965 30 46 45.

Let's get out into nature and see the marvels that the Moors left behind. El Palmeral in Orihuela is a charming palm grove, next to the San Anton neighbourhood. Look at the terraces where different plants were cultivated including the palm trees which created a craft industry for making baskets as well as sweets containing dates. Living here are many species of birds as well as rodents and genets. Here you'll also find the Santa Matilde furnace dating from 1888, where they obtained mercury from cinnabar. You'll also find five mines from the 11th century where iron, copper and mercury were exploited.

Chapter 7: Why does Alcoy hail St George?

St George was certainly a very busy, brave fellow, wasn't he? The famous dragon slayer became England's patron saint in 1350. Legend has it that he slayed the fire-breathing creature on top of what is now known as Dragon Hill, near the Uffington White Horse, in Berkshire.

He's also a hero in parts of Spain. The Catalans made him their patron saint in the 15th century for saving a princess by killing a dragon. A rosebush grew out of the dragon's spilt blood and St George, astride his white horse, offered one of its beautiful roses to the grateful young lady. What a romantic!

Prior to that, in the 13th century, the legend saved the beautiful inland town of Alcoy, known as the city of bridges. They too made him their patron saint and celebrate St George's Day on 23rd April but with far more aplomb than the English. While the English may wave a few flags and eat scones with strawberry jam and cream washed down with a lovely cup of tea, the Alcoyanos recreate the mother of all battles.

It may be more than 700 years since St George and his trusty white steed saved the Alcoyanos from surrendering to the Moors but they will always remember him. Although no dragons were involved in the miracles of St George in Alcoy, he still had his work cut out.

Come with us as we weave our way through the mountains to Alcoy. Let's travel back to 1276 for the famous Battle of Alcoy.

Boom! Boom! Boom! The rumbling came nearer and nearer. Louder and louder. Faster and faster still. Although a black cloud was hanging over young José, a farmer boy from Alcoy, unfortunately, for him there was no thunderstorm approaching. This was the sound of 1,000 horses galloping through the Sierra Mariola and hurtling towards his beloved home city. Each horse carried a fearless Moor with one thought on his mind - to take Alcoy to add to his long list of conquests. Who could guess how many men were following on foot to ensure no-one escaped, no-one fled to the next town to warn them that the blue-eyed sultan Al Azraq and his men were on their way.

José shuddered as if a bolt of lightning was hurtling down his body. He stiffened and straightened up. He hoped none of the Christian soldiers beside him felt his fear. His helplessness. They'd been drilled on what to do if the Moors attacked. They'd gone over it so many times that he pictured it in his dreams. But this was real. Plus Al Azraq was leading the army. He was legendary throughout Spain for his fearlessness. For the fact that he never lost. He never surrendered.

"OK, you know what to do. First line, get ready to move forward. See off our unwanted guests. And make sure they never come back." The command had been given. Battle was about to commence.

José felt down his left leg to check his sword was in place. He quickly patted his saddlebag where he'd placed his sharpest axe. Then, with a quick word of assurance in his stallion's ear, he waited for his turn to move forward and fight.

There were two hours before dawn broke, bringing welcome warmth and rays of light so the Alcoyanos could see the enemy they faced. But on this moonless night, there weren't even any shadows to give away the Moors and their hiding places. All they could do was rely on their ears and their horses, who flattened their ears flat against the side of their heads when they sensed danger approaching.

After 30 minutes, José wished he didn't rely so heavily on his ears. The sounds curdled his stomach. He could handle the clash of steel upon steel. And the constant Boom! Boom! Boom! of the cannons. It was the high-pitched screams of men that frightened him and that lived on in his nightmares for many years afterwards.

"Aaaargh," screamed all around him, it felt like an echo. "Aaaaargh," meant someone was wounded. "Aaaargh," Flump! meant someone was so badly wounded – or worse – that they'd fallen from their horse.

He heard someone whimpering non-stop and was embarrassed to realise the noise was coming from him. He bit down hard on his lip to stop himself from making such a racket. He bit so very hard, he made his lip bleed. The whimpering stopped. What he was unable to stop was the constant shaking, the fear, his sheer terror.

Although José had been wishing for dawn to help light his way, when it arrived, he wanted to close the curtains and make it night again. He saw Alcoy was losing the battle. And losing badly.

Nothing short of a miracle would save them now. "Dear

Lord, I beseech you. I'll do anything. Give anything to be able to go home to my dear mama, see her warm smile and hear her tell me to sit closest to the fire as she pushes a bowl of warm lamb stew into my lap," he murmured to himself. He shut his eyes tight, praying harder and faster than he had ever done in his life. He prayed so furiously that the words stuck in his throat and he feared he would choke. He gagged and opened his eyes. He blinked hard. Blinked again. And then he stared in disbelief.

There on the city walls was the biggest white horse he ever did see. It stood 60 hands tall at least. On top of the biggest horse sat the hugest warrior with steely eyes matching his silver armour. The giant placed the biggest arrow José had ever seen into a massive bow and drew back his arm. He turned away from José and fired into the heart of the Moorish army.

They panicked and scattered every which way in the hope of getting out of the way of this giant deadly weapon with a razor-sharp point. Well, wouldn't you if a world record-breaking arrow was hurtling towards you? There was a severe outbreak of pandemonium in the Moors camp which spread like the most contagious bout of measles.

They weren't sure if turning their backs on the Alcoy giant and fleeing was a wise thing to do. But they did it any way.

Within minutes the thunderous sound of horses' hooves as the Moors retreated became a mere murmur. Then, a welcome silence. They'd gone. Alcoy had defeated Al Azraq and his many men against all the odds.

Who was this miracle man, the saviour of Alcoy? Well, the date was 23rd April and it was evident, to those who followed the stories of the saints, that it was the great St George.

Well, it's no wonder that Alcoy made St George their patron saint. Boy, do they celebrate his special day in style. Every year, from around 21st to 24th April 21, the city once again throbs with the sound of gunpowder and battle cries during the annual Moors and Christians fiesta. This fiesta is so magnificent, it is one of the finest throughout Spain and attracts many thousands of visitors to watch the 5,000 participants act out the great Battle of Alcoy. Each year, St George too makes an appearance on horseback when he fires his arrows from a specially-built castle in Plaza de España square.

Come and witness this marvellous spectacle for yourself. Imagine you are young José, an ordinary Alcoy lad, ready to fight for his beloved homeland and his loved ones.

Who today would be prepared to face a mighty opponent to fight for their home, their freedom and their family?

Who still believes in miracles and the power of prayer?

Could such a miracle as St George really have saved Alcoy or is there a more mundane explanation, such as shadows playing tricks?

Is there always a realistic explanation for everything or are some things beyond or above reason?

We'd advise you to rent a seat along the route for the best views and to avoid standing for hours while the enormous battle takes place. For tickets phone +34 965 54 05 80 or go to www.ticketmaster.es to make the reservation. Also make sure to book your hotel room in or around Alcoy well in advance.

If you can't get to see the Moors and Christians fiesta in Alcoy, there are plenty of other great reasons to visit this old inland Alicante town. The drive into Alcoy is spectacular for a start. In a moment, you'll discover other things to do in Alcoy. First, let's hear about how St George saved Alcoy's neighbour (we told you he was a busy fellow!).

Just 20kms around the Sierra Mariola mountain is the little village of Banyeres de Mariola, which also has St George as its patron saint. It's strange that this tiny mountainous spot boasts a relic of St George within its walls, which is commemorated with a fiesta in the first weekend of September. The annual Moors and Christians event is usually held from 22nd to 25th April, coinciding with St George's Day of course. Every three years, the Legend of St George is dramatised in Vila Rosario park during July – and it's huge! The next performance, due to be held in 2021, will have more than 350 participants creating an amazing show of live music, dance, fire including the flames of the dragon, and special effects.

Now let's take a look at Alcoy, the amazing city of bridges.

Chapter 8: Visit Alcoy, city of bridges

Tucked away among the mountains, Alcoy (Alcoi in valenciano) is famous for putting on one of the most spectacular Moors and Christians fiestas throughout Spain. It's also known as the city of bridges for its magnificent wrought-iron bridges over its river and ravines. Enjoy the 360° far-reaching views across the city, Sierra de Mariola mountains and the Font Roja natural park. This is the perfect stop-off for lovers of natural beauty, history, gastronomy, culture, architecture and Spanish fiestas.

Things to do in Alcoy

Get ready to visit great treasures including two iconic Modernist buildings so impressive that Alcoy is part of the Art Nouveau European Route set up to promote and protect Art Nouveau heritage. These buildings stand as a legacy to Alcoy's industrial and economic importance at the start of the 20th century. In fact, this city was a pioneer of the Spanish Industrial Revolution and the first place in the world to make cigarette papers for rolling tobacco in the early 19th century. As if that wasn't enough, Alcoy is also the birthplace of the most famous tapas in the world - stuffed olives! Oh, and another claim to fame, is that the oldest Three Kings Parade in the world just happens to be in Alcoy.

As you're about to see for yourself, this gorgeous city surrounded by magnificent natural beauty has many jewels to her crown.

First, head to the Circulo Industrial building whose facade and interior scream Modernism. This protected building is in the historic heart of Alcoy in Calle de San Nicolas, just 200 metres from the Plaza de España, where we'll be heading soon. Take your time to look at its impressive combination of geometric, animal and vegetal elements such as floral ornaments and female Hellenistic figures.

A few doors down in the same street is the amazing La Casa del Pavo (the house of the turkey), once the studio of 19th century artist Fernando Cabrera. Marvel at the intricate wrought-iron work and mosaics. Don't miss the turkey on the door lintels.

Now let's continue down the street to the grand Plaza de España. This elegant Spanish square provides a fine backdrop to Alcoy's fiestas, including the Moors and Christians fiesta in

April. At Christmas, a giant statue of a King sitting on top of his golden throne takes centre stage in the square. Giggling children love clambering up the statue to sit on the King's lap, no doubt asking him to pass on to Santa what gifts they'd love for Christmas, as well as having their photos taken. We'll find out more about how magical it is to be in Alcoy at Christmas when we visit the Casal de Nadal Christmas museum.

Alcoy's Plaza España is an interesting mix of old and new architecture. You have the magnificent Santa María church, originally built in Baroque style in the 18th century but destroyed during the Spanish Civil War. It was replaced by this wonderful new church with its blue-tiled dome and magnificent bell tower built in a Classicist style from 1940 to 1954. Take a look inside to see the Gothic table in the Communion Chapel and the beautiful mural by Alcoyano painter Ramón Castañer by the main altar.

Iglesia de Santa María, Plaza de España, is open for visits: Monday to Friday 12.00-13.00.

The square is also home to the elegant Neoclassic town hall. Take a look inside to see works of arts by famous painters such as Antoni Miró, Fernando Cabrera Cantó, Ramón Castañer,

Adolfo Dura, Plácido Francés, and Edmundo Jorda.

The ayuntamiento (town hall) is open: Mondays to Thursdays 08.00-20.00 and Fridays 08.00-15.00. August opening hours are 08.00-15.00.

Go beneath the square to see an amazing modern building, the Llotja de Sant Jordi exhibition centre designed by Valencian architect Santiago Calatrava, whose iconic work, particularly his bridges, can be seen all over the world. If you've time, take a day trip to Valencia to visit the beautiful City of Arts and Sciences, lovingly designed by Calatrava.

As you go underground into the immaculate white rooms, you may feel like Jonah when he was swallowed by the whale. The centre is designed like the skeleton of a large animal. The main entrance is the animal's tail with the head at the opposite end, so you feel as though you're walking straight into the animal's belly.

The Llotja de Sant Jordi exhibition centre is open: Tuesdays to Saturdays 11.30-13.30 and 17.30-20.30, Sundays 11.30-13.30. Closed in August and when exhibitions are being set up.

Go behind the church to the antique Placeta del Carbó,

which was the centre of medieval Alcoy. There's the grand 16th century Renaissance-style palace, now the Camil Visedo Moltó archaeological museum. Just by the Río Molinar in Carrer Sant Miquel is the MAF (Museo Alcoyano de la Fiesta) Alcoy Moors and Christians fiesta museum. This is the next best thing to actually seeing the fiesta as you get a close-up look at the elaborate costumes and the very essence of this amazing event.

MAF Alcoy Moors and Christians fiesta museum is open: Tuesdays to Saturdays from 10.00-14.00 and 16.00-19.00; Sundays and fiesta days from 11.00-14.00. In July it is open Tuesdays to Fridays from 10.00-14.00 and 16.00-19.00; Saturdays from 10.00-14.00; Sundays and fiesta days from 11.00-14.00. In August it is open from Tuesdays to Saturdays from 10.00-14.00, Sundays and fiesta days from 11.00-14.00. Closed 12th to 26th August.

Still heading towards the river, it's time to step inside the magical Casal de Nadal, found in the old Virgen de los Desamparados chapel in Placeta De La Mare de Deu. Relive the amazing spectacle with which Alcoy celebrates Christmas, particularly the oldest Three Kings Parade in the world! There's also the Pastoretes children's parade taking place on the Sunday before 5th January. Dating back to 1889, the children dress as shepherds to take part in a parade, giving out candies and papers with hallelujahs. With their flock, they go to the stable to meet the baby Jesus. If you wish it could be Christmas every day, this charming museum is the place to visit.

Casal de Nadal, Placeta De La Mare de Deu, is open: Tuesdays and Thursdays 10.00-14.00; Wednesdays and Fridays 16.00-18.30; Saturdays 10.30-14.00; Sundays, fiesta days and the Monday before fiestas from 11.00-14.00.

Next, take a look at Alcoy's most emblematic bridge with its vast arches and amazing views, the Puente de San Jorge (Pont de Sant Jordi in valenciano), in the street of the same name.

Puente de San Jorge in Alcoy, city of bridges

This Art Deco style bridge by architect Victor Cune was built between 1925 and 1931, stands 42 metres above the Riquer riverbed, and is 156 metres long.

Let's now head back up Calle de San Nicolas and past our Modernist buildings to the scenic Glorieta park with a gazebo, pond, flowers and trees giving much-needed shade in summer. Alcoy's oldest park, which opened in 1836, is a peaceful haven to enjoy a rest by the gorgeous gazebo or pond to watch the antics of the ducks and geese.

From here, it's 700 metres to the Refugio de Cervantes in Calle Els Alzamora, one of more than 25 air-raid shelters where the Alcoyanos protected themselves against aerial attacks during the Spanish Civil War. This underground shelter is more than 100 metres long and has an exhibition reliving harrowing testimonies of people who lived through the raids on their city.

Refugio de Cervantes, Calle Els Alzamora, is open: Tuesdays and Thursdays 10.00-14.00; Wednesdays and Fridays 16.00-18.30; Saturdays 10.30-14.00; Sundays, fiesta days and the Monday before fiestas from 11.00-14.00.

Last, but certainly not least, 2kms from the centre of Alcoy is the Serpis museum, home to the world's most famous and most munched tapas. You can observe the whole process of stuffing and packing the olives as well as learn about the history of Serpis. At the end, you can buy a selection of stuffed olives from the Serpis store. Yum!

Museo Serpis, Carretera Banyeres Km2, is open: Monday to Friday 09.00-14.00. Closed fiesta days and from 6th to 19th August.

Places to visit near Alcoy

Alcoy is surrounded by natural beauty with El Carrascal de la Font Roja natural park and the Sierra de Mariola mountain on the doorstep.

The Font Roja park has provided rich pickings over time and you can see evidence of how this land was cultivated - the carboneras for producing charcoal, old lime kilns and the cultivated land on the mountainside. You can also see houses and stables as well as the snow houses where snow and ice were stored and used for gastronomic or medicinal purposes. The Font Roja natural park is a protected area, superb for blissful hiking. The routes are all well-signposted but you are forbidden to move off these paths. Camping is allowed if you get the necessary permit from the Espai Jove de Alcoy (965 53 71 41).

In the interpretation centre you can find information about the park along with the flora, fauna and wildlife you may come across such as ash, maple, olive and oak trees as well as aromatic and medicinal plants. You may come across eagles, owls, lizards, wild boar, badgers, weasels and wildcats.

While here, visit the impressive Santuari de la Verge dels Lliris (Sanctuary of the Virgin of the Lilies) hermitage paying tribute to the miracle of 1653 when the image of the Mother of God appeared on wild lily bulbs. According to the legend, on 21st August 1653, the priest of Confrides found some white lilies while he was praying. Upon closer examination, he saw that in their bulbs were images of the Virgin Mary. Since then, a pilgrimage is held, usually on the third Sunday in September, to celebrate this miraculous event.

The Sierra de Mariola has a long history of human occupation with archaeological finds dating back to Neolithic, Bronze and Iberian times. Beautiful cave paintings believed to be up to 7,000 years old have been found at La Sarga but nowadays they are fenced off to protect them. There are guided visits on specific dates of the year, organised by Alcoy town council and the archaeological museum.

The Sierra de Mariola is a botanist's delight. It is home to a unique collection of more than 1,200 plant species, many of which are used in medicine or gastronomy as well as for making the local fiery hierbas liquor, and perfumes. Look out for the famous Mariola sage as well as fragrant herbs like thyme, rosemary, and lavender.

You may stumble across various reptiles such as lizards, snakes, frogs and toads as well as birds like finches, partridges and robins.

How to get to Alcoy

It's definitely worth driving for this leg of the journey because it's so absolutely gorgeous and there are many places to stop off and visit. Plus the train or bus journey takes a lot longer and you won't get the benefit of stopping where the fancy takes you.

For this part of the journey, we're heading into the beautiful interior. You'll go past stunning mountain ranges, quaint little Spanish villages and glorious countryside on your way to historic Alcoy. From Alicante it takes at least 45 minutes and you can do it as a round trip. On the way to Alcoy, you can drive on the A31 and go through the little towns of Novelda - famous for its vineyards and the Sanctuary of Santa Maria Magdalena, a marvellous example of Spanish Art Nouveau, and with a remarkable resemblance to the more famous Sagrada Familia in Barcelona. - and Elda - famous for its shoe-making industry. You then drive around the Sierra del Maigmó mountain and up to Alcoy. On the return trip, you can head down the faster N340 through the little toy-making town of Ibi and around the other side of the Maigmó mountain.

If you're heading on to Jalón for the next part of our amazing journey, you'll enjoy another country drive taking you to the emblematic Castell de Castells high in the mountains. Castell de Castells is famous for Els Arcs, an enormous natural arch, which makes for stunning photos and is three kilometres from the village. Five kilometres from Castells are ancient cave paintings at Pla de Petracos, believed to have been painted more than 5,000 years ago. So, as you've gathered, this is a marvellous place to stop off en route to Jalón.

What's the weather like?

The hottest months are July and August with a maximum temperature of around 29.5°. The winter months can be cold and you may even see snow, especially on the mountains. The average temperature in January and February is around 8°, falling to just above 3° at night. Spring and autumn are lovely times to visit as the temperatures are warm with an average temperature of 12.9° in April and 16.5° in October. However, you'll see more rain in inland Spain than on the coast. The heaviest rainfalls are from September to December with October having the heaviest rainfall of around 74mm.

Best time to visit Alcoy

Fiesta time! Alcoy's fiestas are spectacular. Book your hotel early though if you decide to come for Moors and Christians in April or Christmas, which starts with the Betlem de Tiristi nativity scene on or around 21st December and ends with the Three Kings parade on 5th January.

If you're coming for the Moors and Christians, it is best to book a seat to ensure you get a good view and do not have to stand for hours. Phone +34 965 54 05 80 or go to www.ticket-master.es to make your reservation.

Any time of year is great for visiting Alcoy, although summer flights to Spain are more expensive. If you're planning on hiking or walking through the natural parks or mountains, then spring and autumn are the best times for you.

What type of place is it?

Many tourists tend to stick to the coast and miss out on beautiful - not to mention unique - inland attractions like Alcoy. You'll find Spanish tourists here. You may also find there's not much English spoken but you can certainly get information in English and English-speaking people at the tourist information office.

What to eat in Alcoy

The typical cuisine in Alcoy is very different to the food you'll find on the Costa Blanca. It's earthier, richer, meatier. Winters can be very cold in Alcoy and the food reflects this. There's a wonderful array of gastronomical dishes including:

- Olleta alcoyano - meat and bean stew
- Arroz caldoso - rice with either vegetables, chicken, fish or seafood
- Gazpacho de Mariola - made with meat, mushrooms, garlic and tomatoes as well as the aromatic pebrella herb from Mariola, a type of thyme
- Bajoques farcides - peppers stuffed with rice, meat and vegetables
- Arrop i tallaetes - rich dessert made with grapes

Don't forget to try the local liqueur, the popular Herbero de Mariola, which they say gives you heat, happiness, strength and medicine. Give thanks to the Moors who created this tasty alcoholic beverage which is still made in a totally artisanal way today, from the selection of herbs to the bottling. You should also try the Café Licor Sinc coffee liqueur made in Alcoy and the Vins del Comtat wines from the nearby mountain region of Cocentaina.

Great places to eat in and around Alcoy

To try typical dishes from Alcoy such as olleta and arrop i tallaetes, we'd recommend Restaurante Pension Mariola in Calle San Antonio 4, Agres. In Alcoy itself is Restaurante Lola, Partida Rambla Alta 98, which also serves traditional food from the region such as olleta and pericana (cod, dried peppers and garlic). You can also try the hierbas liqueur or coffee liqueur after a meal.

Restaurante Sant Francesc 52, in the street of the same name and next to the San Mateo church, is a place to sample Alcoyano gastronomy alongside innovative dishes. We'd suggest opting for one of the fixed-price menus or the menú tradicional, full of traditional local dishes.

Another 'out-of-town' restaurant that's just adorable is Restaurante Masía La Mota in Ctra. Font Roja Km 5, in a beautiful boutique hotel. Here the food is a fusion of tradition and creativity using fresh, local produce. There's a good selection of vegetarian dishes and meals suitable for people with diabetes or gluten intolerance. The hotel is in a beautiful setting between the Sierra de Mariola mountains and the Font Roja natural park.

Where to stay?

We love Hotel Masía La Mota as mentioned above. For central Alcoy hotels, the Hotel Sercotel Ciutat D'Alcoi and the Savoy are both lovely hotels in picturesque locations.

How long should I spend here?

At least a day. There's a lot to see and we'd definitely recommend you stay for lunch or dinner because it's such fantastic regional food.

What to photograph that will look amazing on Instagram?

- The impressive arches of the San Jorge bridge. Use the giant pillars of the Viaducto Canalejas to frame a photo over the town to the mountains.

- A selfie with the giant king at Christmas-time.

- The lovely duck house in the Glorieta park.

- Loads of pictures of the Moors and Christians fiestas if you're lucky enough to be in Alcoy at the time.

Secret Alcoy

We have to share this curious fact about Alcoy. There is a saying in Spain "tener mas moral que el Alcoyano" - to have more morale than a person from Alcoy, meaning to talk about a team or a person who never throws in the towel. Its origins are unclear but one theory is that in 1948 Alcoy football team were losing a Cup match by many goals. Presumably to spare them from further humiliation, the referee blew the whistle to end the game a minute early. The Alcoy players pleaded to keep on playing, they maintained morale and blind faith in an impossible comeback. Others say Alcoy were losing 13-0 in a league game but kept on believing they could pull off a victory. The club itself says it does not refer to an actual match but defines their fighting spirit.

Now let's go on a beautiful journey through inland Alicante to a wondrous landscape of mountains and valleys.

Chapter 9: Why is Jalón full of almond blossom?

Every February, the Jalón Valley, also known as the Vall de Pop, is covered in beautiful white blossom as the almond trees wake up to herald the arrival of Spring. The stunning sight of beautiful almond trees in bloom has inspired artists, photographers, writers and poets throughout the centuries. Even Vincent Van Gogh turned his back on his famous sunflowers for a while to paint Almond Blossom as a gift for his brother.

Nature lovers enjoy the incredible views as they walk through fields seemingly painted white to celebrate Spring's arrival. The Jalón Valley is a producer of quality almonds for cakes, pastries and the famous Christmas turrón. But who decided to plant thousands of almond trees in the beautiful Jalón Valley? And why? Imagine facing a valley full of almond trees in blossom with the imposing mountains as your backdrop. Close your eyes and see what these delicate white flowers remind you of? Have you guessed? Let's see if you're right. Come and meet Sultan Ibn Almundin and his beautiful wife Gilda.

"Who is she? Bring her to me," Sultan Ibn Almundin's voice

boomed across the valley and echoed around the mountains. The strong conqueror sat confidently astride his horse. No-one would ever have believed he was nervous, except his mother, who smiled slightly to herself.

The Sultan's long black plaited hair swung across his shoulder as he jumped down from his horse. His dark eyes darted to the left and then to the right until they fixed on the beautiful slave being brought to him, flanked by two of his soldiers. Her eyes were downcast. She dared not look up. For the Sultan was a powerful man who ruled much of Spain and Portugal. She'd done nothing wrong. What could he want with her? She was but his slave. Snatched from her homeland far, far away. For the Moor had conquered her homeland and taken all the local families to be his slaves. Those who survived, that is.

"What is your name?" whispered the Sultan gently. "Gilda," replied the slave girl, who still did not dare look at the great man, although she thought he seemed kindly towards her. She was trembling like a frightened little wild rabbit trapped between two hunting dogs. But then she thought of her home and froze.

"I need to get through this. Hopefully I can find some way

home," she thought and inwardly cried. The Sultan's voice broke into her thoughts.

"You're travelling with me," he told a very surprised Gilda. For the Sultan, it was love at first sight. He'd never seen such beauty or anyone so fair. Gilda came from a cold land, thousands of kilometres north of Jalón. She truly was a fair maiden with hair like spun cotton falling in waves down to her waist. When she glanced up at him, he saw her eyes were the lightest blue albeit tinged with a hint of sadness.

They travelled together for many hours and by the time they arrived at his castle, night had fallen. It was so dark that Gilda had no idea of the splendour awaiting her.

Come the morning, she was summoned before the Sultan again. "We are to be married," he told her. Well, what the Sultan wanted, the Sultan got. In a rather hastily-arranged ceremony, without much pomp or circumstance, she became his wife.

He was kind to her and her life was full of riches. Only the finest sweetmeats and wines passed her lips. She was grateful and even managed to enjoy her new life in many ways.

In spring, Gilda turned her face to the sun and breathed in the heady scent of orange blossom. In summer, she danced and played games with the children of Jalón. In autumn, she loved getting out her paintbrushes and drawing the mountains on to delicate yellowing leaves. But in winter, Gilda turned as pale and as silent as a ghost. She was sadder than a caged canary forced to watch other birds flying free and high into the blue skies.

Gilda enjoys the heady scent of blossom in Jalón

This made the Sultan sad too. And when he was sad, he got angry. "What is wrong with my Gilda?" he asked his advisers. But they could not tell him. He was even desperate enough to ask his mother. But she couldn't tell him either. He was none the wiser when he asked his new wife.

"Nothing is wrong. What could possibly be wrong?" she replied in a whisper that grew fainter and fainter each time he pleaded with her to tell him how he could make her happy and smile again.

Behind the Sultan's broad and muscular back, his court started calling Gilda, the Ice Queen. She was as cold as the iciest winter in Southern Spain's Sierra Nevada. She was as silent as snowflakes falling to the ground.

One day, after a sumptuous feast of roasted lamb and figs, the Sultan demanded to know what was making Gilda so miserable.

So she told him.

"I miss my country," she blurted out as huge tears started pouring like waterfalls down her fair cheeks.

"In spring, we celebrate because the bare trees suddenly spring forth with pink and white blossom. In summer, we enjoy feeling the warm sunshine on our faces as we work outdoors, in the greenest fields. Then, when the leaves dry up and fall to the ground to provide a thick golden carpet to walk upon, we work hard to harvest the food and prepare for winter."

Gilda stopped. She gulped twice like a goldfish fighting for breath. The tears fell faster and faster as she looked the Sultan in the eye, took a deep breath and confessed: "I miss winter so much. There wasn't so much work to do so we could go skiing and skating on the frozen lakes, laugh as we walked and saw how huge our footprints were in the deep, white snow. And as we laughed, our breath would freeze in front of our faces. Which made us laugh even more."

The Sultan was taken aback. How could anyone love the cold, the ice, the frost? A shiver ran up and down his spine just thinking about it. For him, it was the warmth of the sun which made him smile.

This wasn't about him though, it was about his beloved Gilda. How could he put the smile back on her enchanting face? It wasn't possible for Gilda to return to her homeland to see snow. That was definitely out of the question after the Sultan had slain many of her townsfolk and taken others, including herself, as his slaves.

So if he couldn't take Gilda to the snow, how could he bring snow to Gilda? Once every 30 years or so, there may have been a smattering of snow in the Alicante region but not to the depth that his gorgeous wife required. Certainly not enough to play in or to ski. And it wouldn't snow each and every winter.

"I've got it," he declared standing up so fast the blood rushed straight to his head. "Be patient with me, my sweetheart. For you shall have snow."

For the next few weeks, the Sultan put his men to work in the fertile valleys in and around Jalón. They worked from sun up to sun down getting the soil ready for planting and digging intricate irrigation channels for which the Moors were so famous. One day as they were toiling in the fields, they heard the thunder of hooves. They looked up to see a long train of mules stopping alongside the fields. They and their handlers had travelled from the Middle East to bring native almond trees all the way to Jalón to plant around the Sultan's castle.

For many, many days, the workers carefully planted the little trees, propping them up with sticks so they didn't fall and break in the windy afternoons. Then they waited. The trees grew taller and stronger, planted in straight rows like soldiers on the parade ground.

Following a fairly mild winter, when the sun started to warm the soil, and the birds sang merrily in the trees, little buds started shooting out on the newly-planted trees. Every day, the

Sultan went to the top of his castle to look out over the valleys filled with almond trees and smiled. One day he climbed to the top and laughed. His heart was filled with joy.

"Gilda," he shouted, his voice booming out over the mountains. He ran to find his wife, sitting quietly with her arms folded in her lap. "Come, now," he ordered, holding out his hand. Gilda put her delicate hand into his and he pulled her to her feet. Together, they raced to the top of the castle and, before Gilda had a chance to catch breath, her husband put his hands over her eyes. He whispered gently in her ear: "It's snowing just for you, my royal gorgeousness."

He took away his hands and Gilda stared. For as far as the eye could see, the almond blossom had transformed the valleys into a dazzling white carpet looking like snow.

Does the blossom in Jalón look like snow to you?

And Gilda smiled for the first time in 73 days. She rushed out to play in the almond orchards with blossom falling daintily into her hair just like fluttering snowflakes from her homeland.

Did they live happily after? What do you think? Gilda was forced to live as a slave after being cruelly snatched from her beloved homeland. Every February when the valley turned white with beautiful almond flowers, she still shed a tear or two for the real snow and fluttering snowflakes that made her laugh so giddily with her friends and family back home.

Shall we reflect on this story a while and ponder on:

Did the Sultan truly love Gilda? If he loved her, would he have freed her so she could return home?

Did Gilda feel trapped? Was she still the Sultan's slave even though they were married?

What would we do for love? Do we go far enough to make other people happy?

Should we bring parts of our homeland to our new country? Or should we totally embrace our new way of life and throw off the old way of life when we move?

Turn to the next chapter to find out more about the beautiful Jalón Valley and things to do when you visit Jalón. Come in early spring, if you want to see how much the blossom resembles snow but the picture-postcard perfect Jalón Valley surrounded by mountains is amazing to visit at any time of year.

You'll want to take hundreds of photos so make sure you have your camera or your phone is well charged with plenty of room for your pictures.

Chapter 10: Beautiful natural attractions in Jalón

Welcome to the wine-making region of the Jalón Valley. It's amazingly beautiful with lush, green mountains and fertile valleys full of fruit trees and vineyards. It makes you wonder how Gilda could have been so sad to live here. It's amazing! But the reason why it's so colourful, vibrant and picture-postcard perfect is thanks to the unhappy Gilda. It was her husband who had all those trees brought over to try to reproduce snow for his lovely ice queen.

Now we are reaping the benefits. The Jalón Valley with its narrow and twisting roads, challenging mountain climbs offering far-reaching views across the valleys have made this a very popular choice for walkers, cyclists and artists.

Spanish writer Gabriel Miró lived in Parcent, one of the Jalón Valley villages, and called it 'a paradise between the mountains'. You'll soon see why he was so impressed.

Things to do in Jalón

We'll start in Jalón itself (known as Xaló in valenciano) where you'll get to know a typical Spanish village surrounded by a backdrop of magnificent mountains. Take a look at the orchards full of citrus fruits, almond trees and vines. Close your eyes and imagine what these trees look like in full bloom. When those delicate clouds of pink and white blossom fill the valleys for a short time in late January or early February.

This is a lovely little village to just wander through. Take a stroll down any of the charming, narrow streets which take your fancy. Marvel at the large doors and interesting brass door knockers on the townhouses. Visit a little bar or shops such as bakers, butchers, honey shops, and bodegas or wine cellars. From many streets you'll enjoy a glimpse of the impressive mountainous backdrop. Others look towards the Iglesia de Santa María, with its distinctive blue-tiled dome.

You'll find plenty of honey in Jalón

During your time exploring Jalón, make sure you head to the main square, the Plaza Mayor, to see the Iglesia de Santa María church built in a Neoclassical style. If you love traditional Spanish street markets, visit Jalón on Tuesday mornings when the streets surrounding the church are filled with stalls selling local produce, food, clothes, pottery and other Spanish handicrafts.

Another fine day to visit is Saturday mornings for the bustling Jalón flea market to buy antiques and second-hand goods. Called a rastro in castellano, this extremely lively market is held in the riverbed car park, opposite Bodegas Xaló. This is where we're heading to next. It's a lovely walk alongside the Gorgos riverbed to the large car park, where the antiques market is held. Across the road is Bodegas Xaló, a temple to wine, olive oil and other delicious local delicacies. This wine co-operative has produced many award-winning wines at very reasonable prices.

Step inside the bodega to see the huge barrels and enjoy a free sample of some wines. Particular favourites are the award-winning white Bahía de Dénia, the red Vall de Xaló and the cava Vall de Xaló Brut Nature, which tastes better than the far-more expensive Champagne in my view. You can also buy olive oil, honey and raisins produced in Jalón.

Bodegas Xaló, Ctra. Xaló-Alcanalí, is open: Monday to Friday 09.30-13.30 and 15.30-19.30; Saturdays from 10.30-14.30; Sundays and holidays from 09.30-13.30.

In the car park opposite the bodega, you'll often see locals selling oranges, lemons, grapefruits and loquats at unbelievably low prices.

Give thanks to the Moors who lived here for turning the Jalón Valley into a very important wine-producing region. According to the Bodegas Xaló website, in 1472 the Muslim farmers from Jalón were the most important suppliers of the muscat grapes to the markets in the Kingdom of Valencia. In the 15th century, Valencian knight Joanot Martorell sought inspiration from Jalón Valley wine while writing his novel Tirant lo Blanch.

Oh little town of Llíber

For more fabulous views over the Spanish countryside, a visit to Llíber has to be on the list.

This little village ticks all the right boxes for people seeking a taste of traditional Spain. Plus you'll be rewarded with far-reaching country views and a glimpse of what life used to be like in Llíber.

In the car park as you enter the village, look out for a large old stone on top of the communal well. This is where farmers and shepherds collected drinking water for their animals while the local women filled their pitchers for cooking.

For such a small place, it has a surprisingly impressive church, Iglesia de San Cosme and San Damián, with a lovely clock tower. Built in the Neoclassical style in 1700, it's truly beautiful, particularly the wood carvings of the two saints. Stroll around the outside of the church to enjoy the traditional facades of the old houses.

You can leave your car in Jalón and walk alongside the Gorgos river to Llíber. It's about 2.5kms and flat, so easily do-able in around 30 minutes.

Serenity in Senija

If you've time, head 4kms east to tiny Senija to drink in wonderful views over the fertile Jalón Valley. Since ancient times, the farmers produced raisins here.

It is still an agricultural area with citrus, olive, carob and almond trees.

Iconic arches of Castell Del Castells

Now we need to get back in the car for the amazing climb up to the iconic Castell de Castells. Make sure you've got your camera or your phone is well charged up because the views are spectacular even by Spain's high standards.

This is ideal walking and hiking country. At the source of the Jalón river and surrounded by mountains, it's a magical space for nature lovers and history lovers. Ancient Neolithic cave paintings believed to have been created more than 5,000 years ago can be found at Pla de Petracos, six kilometres from Castells. It's one of the most outstanding examples of the Macroschematic post-Paleolithic rock art style in Europe.

You can visit Pla de Petracos site at any time. From Castell de Castells, drive along the CV720 and Camí a la Vall d'Ebo road.

While here, get a picture of yourself next to one of most photographed images of the region, Els Arcs, an impressive enormous natural arch about 900 metres above sea level, six kilometres from Castell de Castells along the CV752. It's a beautiful hike through the mountains too, with your efforts amply rewarded by far-reaching, panoramic views along with peace and solitude.

Beautiful, bountiful Benigembla

Now we can head down the mountain for a 15-minute drive to little Benigembla, home to around 400 villagers. Like Senija, this area's wealth previously came from the raisin trade. As you stroll around, you'll see the 18th century Neoclassical Parish Church of San José, and the three-metre-high town wall built in 1958 to defend the village from the River Xaló. At the turn of the 20th century, as many as 40 homes disappeared in a landslide caused by the surge of the river water, thus the need for a strong wall.

You'll also see the communal laundry where the locals did their washing many years ago and typical riuraus which are traditional buildings used for drying the grapes to produce raisins. These were transported to Dénia where they were shipped all over Europe.

This pretty little place still makes use of its riverside location with various fountains still being used today - Font de Baix, Font de Dalt, Font del Ullet, Font de Murtetes and Font de Pascualest.

Medieval Murla

When you stand in Murla, it's incredible to think how important this little place was during the Middle Ages. In the 16th century, this was the only village in the Marina Alta area which had a Christian population. They played a vital role in resettling people in the surrounding towns and villages when the Moors were banished in 1609.

Notice the decorative iron balconies on the buildings, interesting bell tower on the Castillo-Iglesia de San Miguel, communal laundry and fountains.

Amazing Alcalalí

Another traditional little Spanish village, Alcalalí is the place to come to learn about the wonderful Jalón Valley's wine and olive industry in the Museo Etnológico, Calle Porche, open Monday to Saturday 10.00-13.00.

But there's a truly wondrous tale to hear in Alcalalí from the Moorish times. Pirates and bandits were continually trying to attack Alcalalí and the wider Jalón Valley, so in the late 14th and early 15th century the ruler of Alcalalí and Jalón, Mosen Pedro de Castellví, ordered a hilltop tower to be built. Its purpose was twofold - as a watchtower to look out for marauders and as a last refuge if they were invaded. In the 16th century, a palatial residence was added with a drawbridge to the tower.

The tower and palace have been completely restored and you can enjoy panoramic views over the Jalón Valley from here.

The original function of the tower was a jail on the ground floor, salon for the lords on the first floor, accommodation on the second and third floors with the watchtower on the fourth floor. On the second and third floors, there are engravings and markings from the 16th to 18th centuries which enable you to learn more about the customs of the people who lived in Alcalalí during those centuries. See these for yourself when you visit the tower, now home to the museum and the majestic viewpoint from the top floor. Can you imagine the views in Spring when all the trees are in bloom?

As you wander around the streets keep an eye out for really ornate door knockers, keyholes, little faces in the gutters and rings for tying the mule or horses.

It's a beautiful little place, which is fiercely proud of its heritage. Indeed, the ancient crafts of lace making by hand and crocheting are still practised and taught to this very day.

Paradise in Parcent

What will you make of Parcent? Is it a paradise between the mountains as Gabriel Miró said? Or has one of the other villages taken your fancy more? It certainly has a lot of competition.

If this isn't paradise itself, then it's certainly pretty close with breathtakingly-beautiful views up to the majestic mountains and out to the Mediterranean.

This is perfect hiking and cycling country. Cyclists can enjoy the challenge of riding up the magnificent mountains and natural parks of the Serrella, Bernia, Cavall Verd and Carrascar to seek out even more legacies of the Moors. Walkers can enjoy part - or all if they're feeling particularly energetic - of the Carrascar de Parcent walking route towards Coll de Rates where you'll be rewarded with even more marvellous valley and mountain views.

This is a marvellous area for walkers, cyclists, photographers, artists and nature lovers. There's so much to take in, so make sure you have plenty of time to just sit, breathe, relax and look around you.

In Parcent itself, you should visit the Iglesia Parroquial de La Purísima Concepción parish church with its unique bell tower completed in 1929 and the communal laundry, near the river where the views are amazing.

Iglesia Parroquial de La Purísima Concepción, Plaza del Pueblo, is open: Thursdays and Saturdays at 18.30; Sundays at 13.00; and also on the first Friday of each month there is a Mass at 19.00.

What else to see while you're here

We'd definitely recommend a trip to Cueva de Las Calaveras cave in Benidoleig. Believed to be around 100,000 years old, this is a fascinating trip for all ages because you'll see all sorts of weird and wonderful shapes in the rocks including a polar bear, a map of Spain, President Kennedy's face and Sophia Loren's bust. Honestly! It's also cool inside so a lovely attraction to visit in summer when it's sizzling hot. Remains dating from the Bronze Age and Neolithic times have been found in the cave as well as spectacular stalactites and stalagmites.

Cueva de Las Calaveras cave, CV733, Benidoleig, is open: all year from 09.00-18.00 in winter and 09.00-20.00 in summer. There is a small entry fee of around €3.90.

While in the area, time permitting, take a trip to the tranquil El Sanatorio San Francisco de Borja, more popularly known as the Sanatorio de Fontilles, Partida Castellet, Vall de Laguar. This old sanatorium for leprosy patients opened in 1909 and developed into a little town with more than 300 patients, a bakery, carpenters, blacksmiths, shoemakers and more. Today it is still a centre of reference in the fight against leprosy.

How to get to Jalón

As you'll be visiting several places, it is best to drive. The roads can be narrow, windy and steep in places but take your time and enjoy the views. From Alicante take the N332 or the AP7 toll road to Benissa and then get on the CV745 through Senija and Llíber to Jalón. It will take just over an hour.

What's the weather like?

Summers will be hot with temperatures easily reaching 30° or more in July and August. Winters are mild with an average temperature of around 10° and 11° in December, January and February. October and November are the rainiest months.

Best time to visit Jalón

Fabulous times to visit are in late January or early February when the trees are full of pink and white blossom. The sight and scent are divine. Throughout February, the Alcalalí In Flower festival is held, dedicated to the beautiful almond blossom, with several guided walks organised, so you can see the blossom trees at their most spectacular.

September and October are also great months for a trip to Jalón at harvest-time. This is prime wine country with some award-winning wines produced right here. In autumn you'll see the tractors – and sometimes horses – pull carts packed with grapes to be turned into super wines.

In winter and spring, the area is very popular with cyclists, including professional cycling teams, who take advantage of the relatively mild weather to tackle the challenging bendy roads and mountain climbs.

What type of place is Jalón?

These are all small villages and hamlets with a traditional Spanish look and feel. That said, a large expat community lives here for its charming beauty. In Jalón itself, there's a population of around 3,300, of whom 970 are British.

Where and what to eat in Jalón Valley?

The food is different to what you'll find on the coast and the Jalón Valley has its own specialities. You'll find a lovely variety of homemade sausages as well as sobrasada (made of pork and paprika), butifarras (like black pudding) and chorizo. Local dishes to try include cocas (mini pizzas with a variety of toppings such as peas or anchovies), arròs amb fesols i penques (rice with beans and thistle artichoke), and espencat with red pepper, aubergine and cod. The local citrus fruits, almonds, raisins and honey are also used to produce rich dishes. For dessert, try the pastissets d'ametla (almond cakes).

Definitely visit Casa Aleluya, in Avinguda Rei Juan Carlos I just a few metres from Bodega Xaló. It's warm, friendly, traditional and has a fine line in tapas or paella. Verd i Vent way up high in the Sierra Bernia has fabulous food served with as much local wine as you can drink. It's worth going for the rustic interior of this historic building and the stunning views alone. Restaurante Pepe in Alcalalí is a firm favourite for the warm welcome, quality of the food and prices.

Where to stay?

You'll find AirBnB places, villas to rent, B&Bs and camping in the Jalón Valley. Camping & Bungalows Vall de Laguar is a scenic place to pitch up. There's a bar and pool plus all pitches have either a sea or mountain view - no extra charge! A beautiful hotel with history is Casa Julia in Parcent run by the Reig-Llobell family who have lived in Parcent for several generations and they also run the restaurant serving amazing traditional home-cooked dishes.

For contrast, you could enjoy a day or two inland and stay in a lovely hotel on the Costa Blanca in and around Moraira, Calpe and Altea. If you really want to treat yourself, the luxurious SH Villa Gadea in Altea is fabulous with great sea views, pools, spa and restaurants. The Hotel AR Diamante Beach in Calpe is another lovely spa hotel. The seafront La Sort hotel in Moraira is beautiful too.

How long should I spend here?

You'll need a long weekend at least. The towns may be small but marvelling at all those amazing views will take up a lot of your time. If you're planning on cycling or hiking, then we'd recommend a few days or a week to be able to fit in a few rides plus sightseeing.

What to photograph that will look amazing on Instagram?

- Everything and anything from the ornate door knobs to the views. I guarantee you'll be taking hundreds of photos in the Jalón Valley.

Secret Jalón

Bodega Maserof is an absolute gem. First you get to drive up the Sierra Bernia mountain. Then you'll enjoy the most amazing views. Plus you get to look inside a traditional house with lots of grand treasures inside. You'll also be drinking wine from the Maserof vineyard and enjoy flamenco with your meal. Go in September if you want to take part in the traditional treading of the grapes to help make that delicious, very more-ish wine.

Go to Forn de Murla bakery in Murla for the most amazing home-made cocas and where the bread is still kneaded by hand.

Chapter 11: How did a famous Biblical relic end up in Alicante?

Think of a pilgrimage in Spain which attracts thousands of participants every year and the Camino de Santiago de Compostela immediately springs to mind. Granted, it's a fantastic thing to do and extremely beautiful. But you have to cover at least 100 kilometres to reach Santiago to get the coveted La Compostela pilgrim certificate and you'll probably have a blister on your feet for each and every kilometre you've walked. Let's head over to Spain's second most popular pilgrimage. It starts in Alicante, ends in Santa Faz, and is only seven-and-a-half kilometres long. Phew!

Firstly, let's hear about why this pilgrimage takes place each spring. We're heading back to 1489 when the Alicante region endured a hard year of drought. No water. No crops. No liquid refreshment for the animals. It was the toughest year that the townsfolk had ever endured. Let's travel back to the 15th century now. Let's go to San Juan, on the outskirts of Alicante city.

Pablo squinted and peered up at the aquamarine blue sky. He squinted even harder. There wasn't a cloud to be seen. He looked North. He looked to the East, South and then West. No fluffy white balls of cloud anywhere. He sniffed with his nose as high in the air as he could manage. There was a faint hint of orange blossom from his neighbour's orchard. He smelled his wife's lamb stew slowly simmering on the fire. But he could not smell rain.

"Hey there Pablo. What are you doing?" asked Father Villa-franca, swaying towards him in his black robes. "Looking for rain," he replied. The priest stood beside him and looked up to the sky too.

"Pedro says his crops haven't tasted rain for a year now," said the Priest. "He's bringing up as much water as he can from the rivers and streams but he fears that won't last much longer. If his crops fail and his horses die of thirst, he doesn't know what will become of him and his family. And he has three young children to feed."

"Talk about stating the obvious," thought Pablo, although it would take a braver man than him to share his thoughts out loud. Every Sunday at Mass the congregation were asked to pray for rain. Every Monday, they woke up to be welcomed by another blue sky. Not a whiff of rain.

"Mmmm, I have an idea. I'll get back to you," said the Priest rather more excitedly than usual. He clasped his hands behind his back and walked off thoughtfully.

Pablo didn't have to wait very long before finding out what the Priest had in mind.

"A procession! What good will come of that?" he muttered angrily as he read this notice on the church door.

"On 17th March, 1489, you are cordially invited to join a procession from San Juan to the Nuestra Señora de los Ángeles shrine where we will be offering up prayers for rain. As it's such an important occasion, we shall be bringing the Holy Relic with us on our journey."

They certainly meant business if they were bringing the Holy Relic, the Veil of Veronica. For such a small place it was indeed an honour to have such an important piece of Christian history within their walls. They had the very veil that Veronica used to wipe Jesus's face as he carried his Cross to his own Crucifixion. How did they know it was the very same cloth? Because it still bore an imprint of his anguished face.

So how did one of the most important relics in the history of Christianity end up in Alicante?

The relic remained in Jerusalem until the 6th century when the Muslims captured the lands. To keep their religious relics safe, they were transferred to Cyprus and then on to Constantinople. However, in 1453 this city was taken by the Turks and the Emperor's sons fled to Rome, taking these relics with them. The Veil of Veronica was passed to Mosen Pedro Mena who had travelled to Rome to be appointed priest of San Juan, Alicante.

Pablo went to church religiously but he admitted to feeling sceptical about whether a Holy Relic joining a procession would bring rain. He felt they might have had more luck performing a rain dance or using sticks to douse for water. Despite his doubts, on 17th March Pablo headed to the church to join the procession.

Leading the way was Father Villafranca carrying the Holy Relic. The Priest held up his hand and they all said a prayer before moving onwards. As they walked, they offered up more and more prayers asking for the heavens to open and deluge them with sweet rain. Onwards they walked, on and on. The pace became slower and slower, until Pablo felt they had come to a complete standstill.

When passing the little ravine of Lloixa, when they were only about a quarter of the way through their journey, a murmur swept through the crowd from the front to the back like an aural Mexican Wave. When it reached Pablo ears, he stopped still in complete shock. The Priest and his cohorts were finding the Holy Relic too heavy for them. It felt as though it is becoming too much for them to bear.

"Maybe the burden of being in charge of a parish without water is too much for them," thought Pablo angrily. "Maybe they realise they can't help us and this is a perfect excuse to give up and turn back."

Another murmur buzzed through the crowds. They became very excited and surged forward towards the priest. This time the murmur brought the most astonishing news.

"The Holy Relic is crying. It's so heavy because it's wet with tears. Honestly, Father Villafranca looked at the cloth in his hand to see why it was becoming so heavy, so burdensome, and he saw a tear drop down the right eye and run down the cheek," was the message being relayed.

By the time Pablo heard the news, a cool wind was whipping up from the East. The sky darkened. Clouds gathered overhead and he heard the pitter-patter, pitter-patter of raindrops hitting hard, parched ground. The procession quickly turned to head for home. Which was just as well as the rain became steadier, faster, harder. And it didn't stop for an entire week.

A monastery has been built in Santa Faz (which means the town of the Holy Face) where the sacred Veil of Veronica is kept. Many thousands of people, including Kings and Heads of States have stopped here to pray at its altar.

Every year, on the second Thursday following Easter Sunday, the Santa Faz pilgrimage is held in memory of the tremendous day when the heavens opened came and broke one year of extreme drought. Each year more than 200,000 pilgrims gather on the morning of the Santa Faz pilgrimage to walk 7.5kms from San Nicolás de Bari cathedral in Alicante to Santa Faz monastery. It may only be a short journey but the pilgrims are well prepared, fortifying themselves with a breakfast of the local sweet mistela wine, anise rolls and thick slices of tortilla – some plain with just egg and potato, others with sweet fried onions too. A hearty breakfast indeed!

The celebrations of the Santa Faz miracle continue over four days with a fairground and market stalls selling typical products from Alicante such as ceramics, along with fresh food and sweets including turrón (nougat), pralines and candy apples. You can even buy religious souvenirs including a replica of the historic cloth. A special Mass is held and this is the only time that people can get to see the Holy Relic, which takes pride of place during the ceremony. For the rest of the year, the cloth is held under lock and key in its own special room behind the main altar.

Part of the mosaic showing the Veil of Veronica in Santa Faz

If you can't join the Santa Faz pilgrimage, you can see the Baroque church at other times, although not the Holy Relic.

Santa Faz monastery, Calle Mayor, 2, Santa Faz, is open: Monday to Saturday 09.00-13.00 and 17.00-20.00; Sundays and fiesta days 09.00-13.00.

Your journey begins and ends in Alicante. We hope you've enjoyed stepping into the historic world of Alicante and following in the footsteps of a few of its legends and miracle makers.

In the next chapter, you can discover a bit more about how the Moors ruled Spain, and the magnificent Moors and Christians fiestas.

Chapter 12: History of the Moors and Christians in Spain

Many things we think of as typically Spanish – rice for paella; golden saffron and other spices such as cinnamon and paprika; oranges; almonds, vineyards and so much more – are actually a legacy of the Moors.

From the moment the Muslim Umayyad dynasty crossed into Gibraltar in 711, the history of Spain changed. Bit by bit, they advanced through Spain taking control of many regions. Their influence is most strongly felt in Andalusia in southern Spain.

They lay the foundations for the European Renaissance bringing their culture, science, philosophy, architecture, decorative arts, farming methods and way of life into the European countries they conquered.

They revolutionised architecture with their advanced irrigation techniques allowing new crops such as citrus fruits and rice to thrive.

But the Christians in Spain were not prepared to give up their kingdoms without a fight. In the 11th century, Christian kingdoms in the north – Catalonia, Aragón, Navarra, Castile and León - slowly started advancing south. Fighting in the name of Christianity, they regained many lands from the Moors

Significant Christian advances were in 1085 when Alfonso VI of Castile gained control of Toledo and in 1094 when the legendary El Cid captured Valencia.

The Christians continued to push south and soon only Granada remained under Moorish control.

The Moorish rule was nearing its end. Their fate was sealed in 1212 during the Christian victory during the battle of Las Navas de Tolosa. However, it took a long time for the Christians to completely take back their lands as Granada was still under Moorish rule until 1492.

This historic period is known as the Reconquista (Spanish for Reconquest) covering from the original Moorish invasion in 711 until their defeat in Granada in 1492 - 781 years later.

All Jews who would not convert to Christianity were expelled from Spain. However, in 1609 King Philip III of Spain demanded the expulsion of all converted Muslims and their descendants.

Now this lengthy period of history is remembered by many

towns and cities during their annual Moors and Christians fiestas. As well as colourful parades, elaborate garments and fireworks, battles between the Moors and Christians are noisily recreated followed by the defeat of the Moors.

Statue of a Moor in costume

Chapter 13: Resources

Tourist Guides

My Guide Alicante online travel guide:
www.myguidealicante.com
Comunitat Valenciana tourist information:
http://comunitatvalenciana.com
Costa Blanca tourist information:
http://www.costablanca.org
Alicante city tourist information:
https://www.alicanteturismo.com
Orihuela tourist board:
https://www.orihuelaturistica.es
Guardamar del Segura tourist information:
http://guardamarturismo.com/
Rojales tourist information:
http://www.rojales.es
Alcoy tourist information:
https://www.alcoyturismo.com
Jalón Valley tourist information:
http://valldepop.novitur.com/

The Legends and Myths

Alicante Castle & The Moor's Face:
https://www.castillodesantabarbara.com
http://comunitatvalenciana.com/actualidad/alacantalicante/noticias/
castillo-santa-barbara-alicante:
The Legend of Armengola:
https://morosycristianosorihuela.com/index.php/ct-menu-item-11/
ct-menu-item-13;
https://www.orihuelaturistica.es/orihuela/web_php/index.php?con-
tenido=descripcion&id_boto=4013
https://www.orihuelaturistica.es/orihuela/uploaded/LALEYENDAe-
dicestudianteESP-ING.pdf
La Encantá:
https://es.wikipedia.org/wiki/Leyenda_de_la_Encantada
http://www.rojales.es/juventud-organiza-la-noche-de-san-juan-noche-
magica-de-la-encanta/
Alcoy and St George:
https://www.spain.info/en/que-quieres/agenda/fiestas/alicante/fiestas_
de_moros_y_cristianos.html;

https://www.alcoyturismo.com/alcoy/web_php/index.php?contenido=-descripcion&id_boto=4040

http://en.comunitatvalenciana.com/what-to-do/festivities/moorish-es-and-christians/alcoy

https://en.wikipedia.org/wiki/Moors_and_Christians_of_Alcoy

Jalón Valley almond blossom:

http://en.comunitatvalenciana.com/taxonomy/term/41837;

http://www.alcalaliturismo.com/portfolio/feslali-alcalali-flor/

Chapter 14. About Me

When she was a little girl growing up in Kent, England, Sarah's grandparents Molly and Hugh Farrell used to take Sarah, her siblings and her cousins on mystery tours. They'd organise a day out but the children didn't have a clue where they were going – until they arrived. Molly and Hugh made the journey a part of the adventure by telling wondrous stories (and feeding their grandchildren copious amounts of Smarties).

That love of travelling and storytelling has stayed with Sarah, along with a passion for reading and writing.

She was a journalist and sub-editor for newspapers in the UK before moving to the Alicante region of Spain in 2005, where she continues to be a writer.

Sarah loves learning new things, which is just as well as she has a lifetime of learning about incredible facts, legends, myths and miracles in her new home country. She launched the Secret Spain Travel Guides to share these amazing stories with like-minded adventurous spirits, yearning to find out more about this beautiful country.

When she's not writing, Sarah loves walking, reading, taking photographs, travelling, eating out, and watching football - she supports Charlton Athletic and Valencia.

Contact Sarah and join the mailing list for the latest Secret Spain news. You'll be the first to know when the next Secret Spain Travel Guides are published by going to: www.secretspain.info

Printed in Great Britain
by Amazon

33142678R00090